Usborne **ART** ideas

# big book of things to Draw

Fiona Watt, Anna Milbourne
& Rosie Dickens

Designed and illustrated by Non Figg,
Jan McCafferty & Antonia Miller

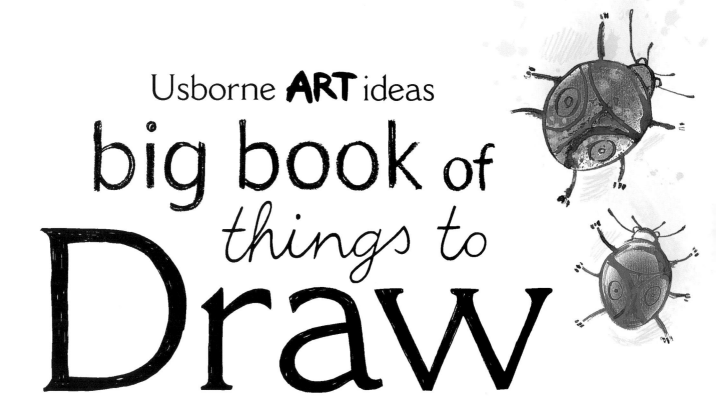

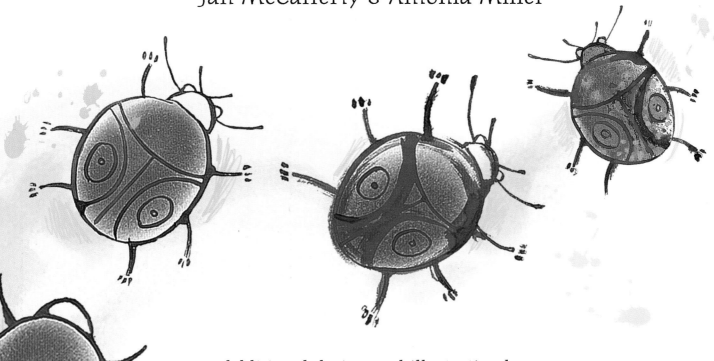

Additional design and illustration by
Doriana Berkovic, Katrina Fearn, Amanda Gulliver,
Catherine MacKinnon, Gary Dunn, Christyan Fox,
John Richardson, Paddy Mounter and Ian McNee

Photographs by Howard Allman

# Contents

 4 Materials

 6 Oodles of doodles

 8 Drawing simple faces

 10 Watercolour giraffe

 12 Domed buildings

 14 Dip pen drawings

 16 Watercolour city

 18 Ink and pastel pets

 20 Inky beetles

 22 Brush and ink drawings

 24 Inky panda

 26 Light and dark

 28 Brush paintings

 30 Head-on hippos

 32 Painting scenes

 34 Animal characters

 36 Adding shading

 38 Shading ideas

 40 Pencil bugs

 42 Drawing with pastels

 44 Oil pastel lizards

 46 Chalky polar bears

 48 A pastel fantasy landscape

 50 Hairy orangutan

52 Oil pastel effects

 54 Wax crayons

 56 Wax resist fish and butterflies

 58 Waxy zebras

 60 Drawing trees

 62 Drawing feathers

 64 Drawing fur

 66 Drawing horses

 68 Kangaroos in motion

 70 Animals in action

 72 Birds in flight

 74 Drawing a face

 76 Shading faces

 78 Dramatic lighting

 80 Drawing side views

 82 Drawing cartoon bodies

 84 Moving bodies

 86 Superheroes

 88 Chasing and racing

 90 Perspective

 92 Skewed views

 94 Drawing from life

 96 Index

# Materials

The techniques in this book use materials which can be found in art shops and most stationers. These two pages give information on some of the materials and how to use them.

## Pencils

Lots of the projects in this book start with a pencil drawing, using lead or coloured pencils. For more details on what type of pencil to use, see pages 36-37.

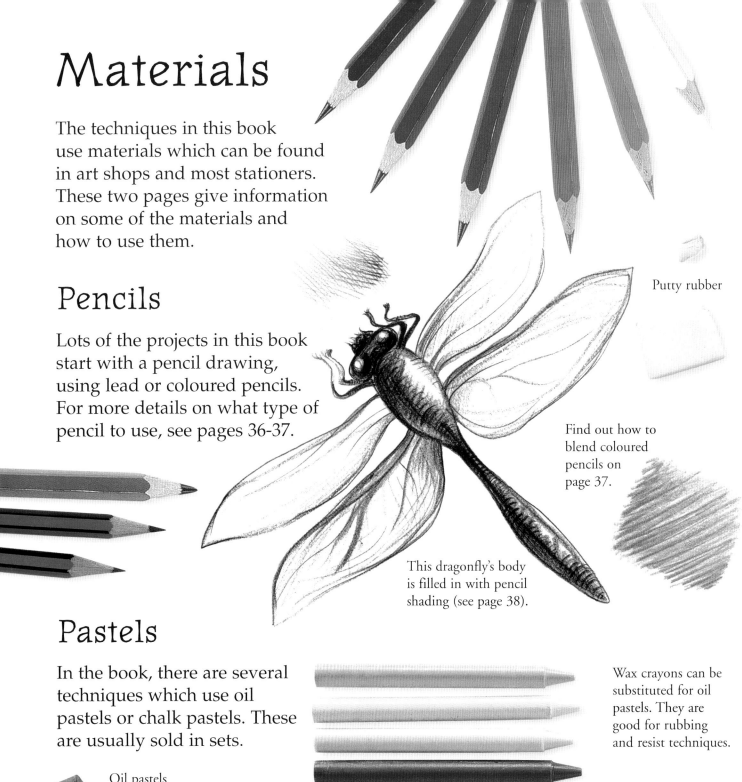

Putty rubber

Find out how to blend coloured pencils on page 37.

This dragonfly's body is filled in with pencil shading (see page 38).

## Pastels

In the book, there are several techniques which use oil pastels or chalk pastels. These are usually sold in sets.

Wax crayons can be substituted for oil pastels. They are good for rubbing and resist techniques.

Oil pastels

Oil pastels give a brighter effect than chalk pastels. Chalk pastels are good for techniques where colours are blended.

Chalk pastels

This tree was drawn with oil pastels.

# Inks

Some of the ideas use coloured inks, which come in bottles. You can also use the ink from a cartridge pen.

# Pens

You'll also need a pen for some of the techniques. Felt-tip pens with permanent ink are ideal as they don't bleed, and they draw on top of most surfaces, including acrylic paint.

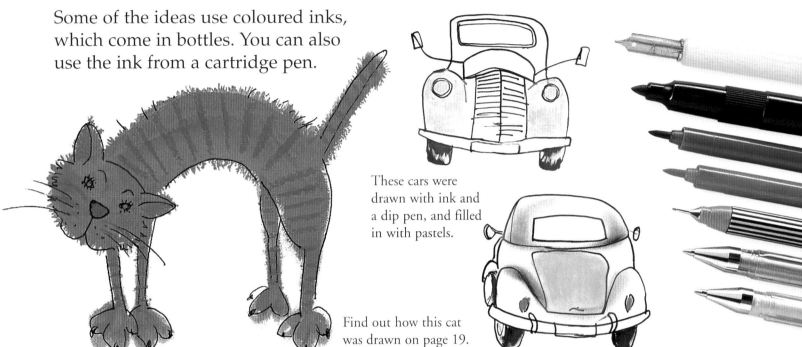

These cars were drawn with ink and a dip pen, and filled in with pastels.

Find out how this cat was drawn on page 19.

# Paint

The types of paint used in this book are acrylic paint, watercolour paint and poster paint.

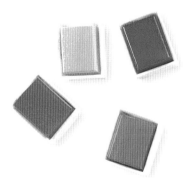

You can buy watercolour paints in tubes or in solid blocks called pans. Mix the paints with water before you use them.

This drawing was filled in with watercolour paints.

5

# Oodles of doodles

Practise drawing by doodling patterns and shapes.

1. Paint lots of different shapes, like these, with red watercolour paint. Flick the bristles of the brush to spatter dots on top, too.

2. When the paint is dry, scribble around some of the shapes with a blue pencil. Add circles, lines and leaves in the spaces.

3. Start doodling lines, circles and dots over the top of the paint and pencil shapes, with a blue ballpoint pen.

4. Then, fill in the spaces between the shapes with lots of wavy lines, circles and squares. Add dots, stars and spirals, too.

5. Carry on doodling around the shapes with the pen, so that you fill most of the paper with different patterns.

6. Then, turn some of the shapes into birds by adding legs, beaks, wings and feathers. Turn some shapes into flowers, too.

You could fill some of the spaces with scribbled blue pencil.

# Drawing simple faces

A simple circle can make a person's face, but it's fun to vary the shape of faces you draw. Experiment with drawing hair, eyes, noses and mouths to give them different characters, like the ones shown here.

## Grinning girl

The ears are level with the nose.

1. Draw a circle for the head. Add little curves for the eyes and nose. Add a semicircle for a mouth.

2. Draw a line across the mouth. Add vertical lines for the teeth. Add ears halfway down each side.

3. Draw lines for pigtails on the head. Draw a few lines for a fringe. Add dots for freckles over the nose.

## Worried man

The tops of the ears are level with the eyes.

1. Draw a long oval for the head. Add circles with dots in them for eyes. Then, add a very long nose.

2. Add an oval mouth. Then, draw a line to join the circles and lines to the sides of the eyes for glasses.

3. Draw two curves for ears. Add little lines for raised eyebrows. Add long lines for hair.

All of these faces were drawn using black felt-tip pen. Then, some parts were added or filled in using coloured felt-tip pens.

# Angry baddie

Add little lines inside the ears.

Add a line above the eyebrows.

1. Draw a curved shape with a flat bottom. Add a line for the eyebrows and a rectangular nose.

2. Draw curves from the nose to the eyebrows, and add dots, for eyes. Draw ears, level with the eyes.

3. Draw a downward curve, for a mouth. Add a smaller one beneath it. Add dots for stubble and lines for hair.

# Cool lady

1. Draw an oval face. Add oval eyes, with a line across each one. Add pupils looking to one side.

2. Add a nose. Draw an 'm' shape and underline it for the top lip. Add a curve for the bottom lip.

3. For the hair, draw a big curve from the top of the head to the bottom of the face, on both sides.

To create this crowd scene, the people at the front were drawn first, then the people further back.

As well as varying the people's faces, try varying the shapes of their bodies, and their clothes.

# Watercolour giraffe

## Painting tips

Watercolour paints come in either tubes, or blocks called pans. Here are some tips on using them.

With pans, rub a wet brush on the pan to get paint on the bristles. Dab the paint onto a saucer.

With tubes, squeeze a tiny blob from the tube onto a saucer, and add water with your brush.

Add more water to make the colour paler.

Wet watercolours blur together.

Let a colour dry before adding the next one if you don't want them to blur.

Watercolour paints are good for adding colour to drawings without hiding the original outline. If you want to draw the outline of something before painting it, you need to use a permanent pen – one which doesn't run when it gets wet. If you don't have watercolour paint, use watery poster or acrylic paint.

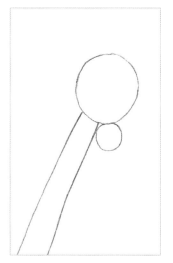

1. Start near the top of the paper. In pencil, draw two circles for the head and two lines for the neck.

2. Draw a triangular body with an oval hip. Add four long stick legs. Put circles halfway down the front legs.

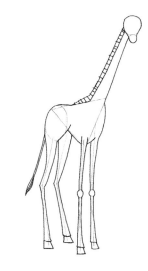

3. Draw the outline in permanent pen. Make the knees knobbly. Add the hooves, a mane and a tail.

4. Add ears, horns, eyes with semicircular eyelids, and curly nostrils. Then, rub out the pencil lines.

5. Draw a low hill and a tree. Mix yellow watercolour with a little red and fill in the giraffe's shape.

The orange splodges will blur on the damp paper.

6. Mix a bright orange. Dab splodges all over the giraffe's body while the paper is still damp.

7. Paint the mane and tail orange, and the hooves and horns grey. Dampen the background a little and paint it. Let the colours blur together.

When the paint is dry, you could add a pen line around the picture to frame it.

You can do all kinds of animals using this technique. Draw quickly. If the lines are a little lopsided it gives the animal more character.

The blurry effect can add to the picture. Here, the pink from the flamingo has spread into the water and looks like a reflection.

Paint a very simple background to make the animal stand out.

# Domed buildings

These colourful buildings were drawn first and then filled in with watercolour paints.

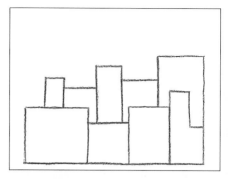

1. Use a pencil to draw several large rectangles on your paper. Make them different sizes.

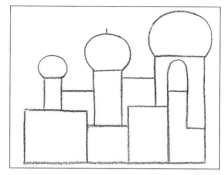

2. Add some domes and turrets. Make them different sizes and shapes, too.

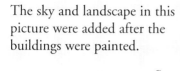

The sky and landscape in this picture were added after the buildings were painted.

3. Add lots of different shapes of windows, doorways, columns and arches to the buildings.

4. Use watercolour paints or inks to fill in the buildings. Leave a small gap between each part.

5. When the paint or ink is dry, fill in the domes with a gold felt-tip pen or gold paint.

6. Draw around some of the windows and add patterns to the buildings with a gold pen.

# Dip pen drawings

These cars were drawn with a dip pen, but you could use a cartridge pen.

Try drawing modern and old-fashioned cars.

This red chalk pastel was smudged with a fingertip.

When you draw with a dip pen, it gives you a slightly uneven line.

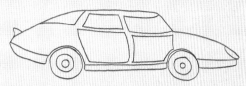

1. Pressing lightly, draw a simple outline of a car with a pencil. You could use pictures from books or magazines to help you.

2. Draw the windows, doors, wheels and hubcaps. Then, add the headlights and rear lights, then the bumpers.

Draw clutch bags and shoulder bags.

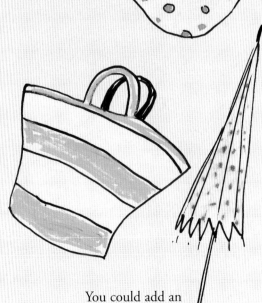

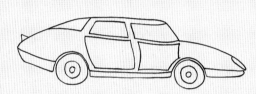

3. Dip the nib of a dip pen into some ink and go over the pencil lines. Dip the pen into the ink each time the nib runs dry.

4. Add details such as door handles, wing mirrors, radiator grills and number plates. Leave the ink to dry completely.

Leave some parts of the cars uncoloured.

5. Draw lots more cars from different views. Do some from the side, some front-on and some from the back.

6. When the ink is completely dry, use chalk pastels or felt-tip pens to fill in different parts on each of the cars.

You could add an umbrella, too.

# Watercolour city

This project works best on thick paper or watercolour paper.

You could paint a taller building above the row of buildings at step 1.

These tiny people make the buildings look huge.

1. Mix different shades of orange, purple and red watercolour paint. Paint a row of buildings, almost touching each other.

2. Mix some light blue watercolour and paint the sky above the buildings. Add darker blue shapes when the sky has dried.

3. Use ink and a dip pen, or a felt-tip pen, to outline the buildings at the front in black. Draw a roof on each one.

Some of the windows in
this picture were filled
in roughly with ink.

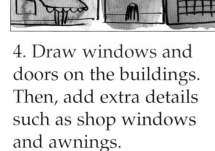

4. Draw windows and
doors on the buildings.
Then, add extra details
such as shop windows
and awnings.

5. Outline the buildings
at the back. Make them
look like skyscrapers by
adding rows of dots and
lines for windows.

6. Draw some pavements.
Then, paint simple shapes
for cars and outline them
when the paint is dry.
Draw some people, too.

# Ink and pastel pets

The ink will run on the paper.

1. Use a clean sponge or a wide paintbrush to wet a piece of watercolour paper.

2. Dip a thick paintbrush into some bright ink and paint lines for the head, ear, body, legs and tail.

3. While the ink is still wet, use the tip of a brush to add spots. Do one on the head for the eye.

Fill in around the dog with another colour of ink.

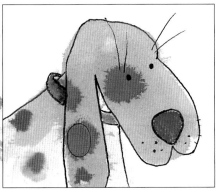

4. When it's dry, outline the body with a black felt-tip pen. Add a nose, eyes and lines on the paws.

5. Draw on a few dots and hairs, too. Fill in the nose and draw a collar with chalk pastels.

In this picture, the
roof was drawn
after the cat.

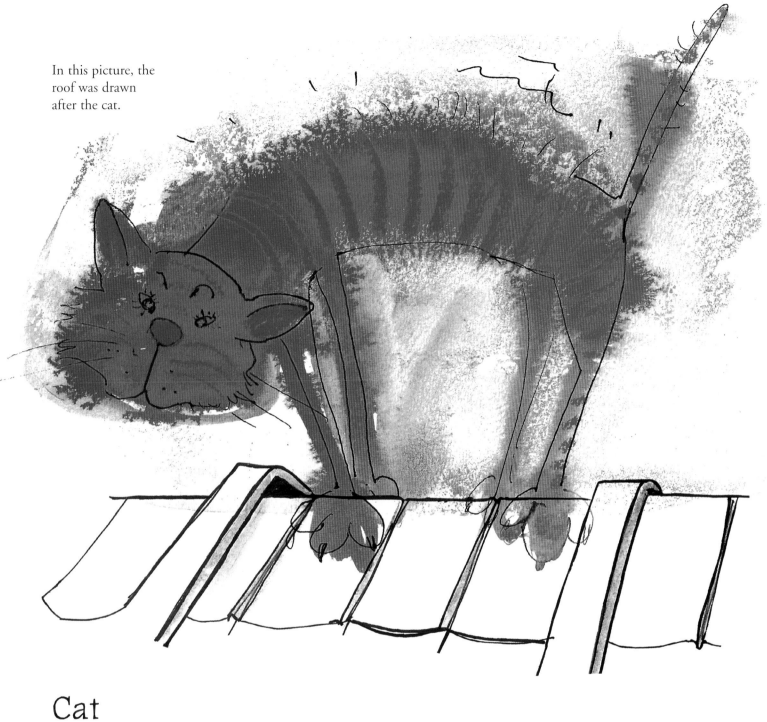

# Cat

Fill in the ears and nose, too.

1. Paint a curve for a cat's
back on wet watercolour
paper. Add a head, legs
and a line for a tail.

2. When the ink is dry,
draw stripes on the
body, legs and tail with
a chalk pastel.

3. Use a felt-tip pen to
draw an outline. Add
claws and whiskers too.
Add eyes with a pastel.

# Inky beetles

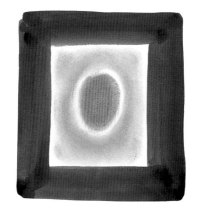

1. Use ink to paint a large rectangle. When it's dry, draw an oval with an orange chalk pastel.

2. Fill in around the oval with blue pastel. Then, use a finger to smudge the pastel over the paper.

3. Dip a thin paintbrush or dip pen into some pink ink and use it to draw a simple outline of a beetle.

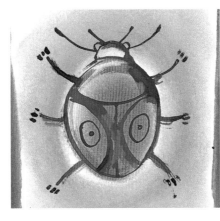

4. Add eyes and feelers to the head. Draw 'toes' at the end of the legs. Add patterns on the wings.

5. While the ink is still wet, smudge it across the the body and along the legs with a fingertip.

6. Put your picture onto a newspaper. Then, flick a paintbrush to splatter ink over the beetle.

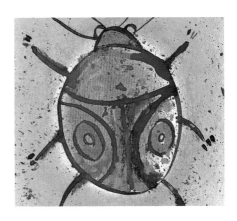

7. Fill in parts on the head, wings and body with a gold pen. Draw pastel dots on the wings.

8. Use a dip pen and ink or a thin felt-tip pen to write around the beetle. Use flowing lettering.

9. Smudge the pastel dots on the body. Then, use pastels and a gold pen to decorate the frame.

21

# Brush and ink drawings

The best kind of brush to use for pictures like these are soft brushes which have a pointed tip. Chinese or Japanese lettering brushes are ideal for these techniques.

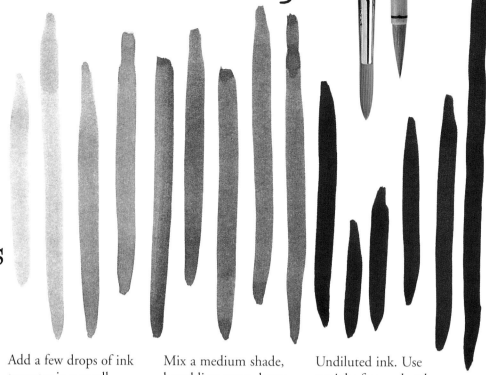

## Mixing the inks

To do the drawings on these pages, you need to use three shades of one colour of ink. Use ink from a bottle or snip the end off an ink cartridge.

Add a few drops of ink to water in a small container to make a watery ink.

Mix a medium shade, by adding more drops of ink to water in another container.

Undiluted ink. Use straight from a bottle or squeeze the ink from a cartridge into a container.

## Bamboo

Practise on scrap paper before doing a large picture.

Use the width of the bristles to paint.

1. Dip your brush in the watery ink, then dab the bristles on a paper towel. Paint a section of a stem.

Don't put more ink on your brush.

2. Paint another two sections above the first one. Leave a small space between each section.

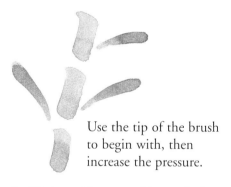

Use the tip of the brush to begin with, then increase the pressure.

3. Using the medium ink and the tip of your brush, add branches coming out from the stem.

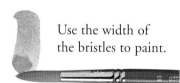

4. Add twigs onto the branches. Leave a small space between one twig and the next one.

Use undiluted ink.

5. For a leaf, press lightly on the tip of the brush, then press a little harder then press lightly again.

6. Use the tip of the brush and undiluted ink to paint grass and lines at the joints on the stem.

# Bird

For each line, start with the tip, then press harder, then lighter again.

1. Using undiluted ink, paint the beak with the tip of your brush. Add the neck and body.

2. Paint the head, an eye and a line for the bird's back. Add a branch at the bottom of the body.

Make the lines different lengths.

3. For a tail, paint several lines joining on to the body.

# Inky panda

You can use a brush and ink to do simple paintings of animals. Using watery and strong shades of two colours can give a striking effect. Use a soft brush with a pointed tip for this type of picture.

1. Mix watery black ink. Paint the panda's head and body, using a smooth, flowing line. Leave it to dry.

Make the paws shaggy around the edges.

2. Use undiluted black ink to paint the ears. Paint a stripe over the chest, then add the arms and legs. Let them dry.

3. Use undiluted black ink on the very tip of your brush to paint little, round eyes and a nose. Leave them to dry.

The patches slope outwards at the bottom.

4. Paint the panda's eye patches in undiluted black ink. Leave a little white circle around each eye.

## Bamboo

Use the side of the bristles, like this.

1. Mix watery green ink and paint a section of bamboo stem. Paint sections above it, leaving gaps between them.

Let the stems dry before adding the leaves in undiluted ink.

2. Use one brush stroke for each leaf. Press lightly with the tip of the brush, then press harder, and then lightly again.

The grass was painted in the same way as the leaves.

The joints on the stems
were painted in undiluted
ink when the stems were dry.

# Light and dark

When light shines on something, the parts facing the light are palest; the parts facing away from the light are darkest. By adding light, medium and dark areas, you can make a drawing look solid.

The light is coming from here.

Lightest area

Medium area

Darkest area

The snails' shadows fall away from the light.

## Smooth blend seal

Rub out the lines that overlap the flippers and tail.

Add some lines to the flippers.

Add dark shading under the body and on the back and tail.

1. Draw a seal shape as shown above. Start with the big teardrop body and then add the flippers, tail and face.

2. Shade the body by pressing lightly with a pencil and filling the shape in. Leave the lightest areas white.

3. Go over the areas you want to be dark, pressing harder. Press more lightly as you reach the medium areas to blend the two.

## Ink-wash fish

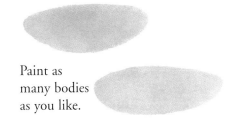

Paint as many bodies as you like.

The two shades will blend together on the damp paper.

1. In a saucer, mix blue ink with lots of water to make a pale shade. Then, paint the oval bodies of the fish.

2. Add more ink to the saucer, and, while the fish bodies are still damp, paint the darker shade on their undersides.

3. When the fish are totally dry, use a blue fountain pen or felt-tip pen to draw their outlines, faces and scales.

In this scene, the sea was painted first, and left to dry. Then, the seals and fish were added.

These seals were painted in exactly the same way as the ink-wash fish.

# Brush paintings

All the pictures on these pages were painted using three shades of ink. You paint the main shapes, then details are added with a very fine brush or dip pen. Before you begin, follow the steps on page 22 for mixing the ink.

## Bugs

1. Use the medium ink to paint a body. Add wings with the watery ink.

2. Add a head, eyes, antennae and legs with undiluted ink.

## Fish

1. Use the very watery ink to paint a simple shape of a fish.

2. Add the head, gills and underside of the fish with the medium ink.

3. Use a pen or fine brush and undiluted ink to add an outline.

4. Add an eye, mouth, fins and a tail with the undiluted ink.

Paint a lily pad with different shades of ink.

For a background like this, paint a watercolour wash. Let it dry before adding the creatures.

Use the tip of a thin brush to paint reeds.

# Frog

1. Use the very watery ink to paint a shape for the body.

2. Use the tip of the brush to add a darker stripe along the shape with the medium ink.

3. Before the body has dried, add some spots of the medium ink to it.

4. Use undiluted ink to draw an eye. Outline the body and add a leg.

# Head-on hippos

Animals look completely different shapes from the front than from the side. Front on, parts of an animal may be hidden by the rest of its body. Its body looks shorter than it actually is. This is called foreshortening.

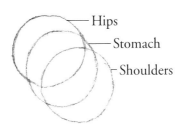

Hips
Stomach
Shoulders

1. In pencil, draw three overlapping circles for the hips, stomach, and shoulders.

2. Draw two circles in front for the head and nose. Add the eyes, nostrils and ears.

3. Draw front legs from the shoulder and a back leg from the hip.

4. Draw the outline, using the circles to show the fat body. Rub out the extra lines.

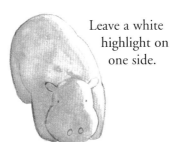

Leave a white highlight on one side.

5. Paint the hippo with brown watercolour paint, making one of the sides darker.

Dab the pink on while the paint is damp.

6. Add a little pink to the mouth and eyes. Let it dry. Draw the outline in fine felt-tip pen.

The grass was painted with green watercolour. When it was dry, the black lines were added using felt-tip.

The background was painted around the hippos before the outlines were added.

# Overlapping shapes

You can use the same shapes to draw the hippo from different angles. You need to overlap the circles more or less depending on which way the hippo is facing.

These body circles spread out horizontally.

These body circles line up diagonally.

These body circles almost totally overlap.

When drawing a hippo from behind, add a small tail.

Some yawning hippos were added to this scene, and the insides of their mouths painted pink.

Lines around the hippos show ripples in the water.

# Painting scenes

There are different ways of painting backgrounds using watercolours. These pages show two ways of painting backgrounds, and also watercolour techniques you can use to make a funny cartoon monster scene.

## Painting backgrounds

Only use a little water.

1. Draw the whole cartoon, including the background detail, using a permanent pen.

2. Paint clean water over the background. This will help you to get an even colour.

3. On the damp paper, paint the background. Paint pale colours before the darker ones.

4. When the background is dry, fill in the foreground, or the main characters.

## Monster moon scene

The colours will blur together.

1. Dampen your paper by painting water onto it or by wiping a damp sponge on it.

2. While it is still damp, mix lots of a very pale colour. Paint it on with a large brush.

3. While the paper is damp, mix a slightly darker shade and paint it on.

4. When the paper is dry, mix a bright colour and paint a blob. The shape doesn't matter.

5. While the blob is damp, add little dots of another colour. They will blur together.

6. When it is dry, add eyes and an outline. It doesn't have to follow the coloured shape.

7. Draw antennae, arms and legs. You can add a tail and other details, such as fangs.

8. Follow steps 4 to 7 to add more monsters. Outline the rest of the background last.

# Animal characters

You can give different animals of one kind, for example cats or dogs, personalities of their own. Vary their expressions and body shapes to create different characters.

These cats were painted with watercolour paint and outlined in felt-tip pen.

## Butch bulldog

1. Draw a circle for the face. Draw a line for the eyebrows and then add eyes. Add a nose, a mouth and pointed teeth.

2. Add curves from the mouth for jowls. Add the body. Then, add stick legs with oval paws, ears and a tail.

3. Outline the legs, tail and ears. Add a patch on its back. Add lines for the wagging tail and draw lines on the paws.

# Snooty pooch

1. Draw a bean-shaped head. Add eyes, a nose and a mouth. Draw a cloud shape for fur, and a line and fur for an ear.

2. Draw a long bean shape for the body and add a cloud shape at the bottom. Add stick legs with paws, and a stick tail.

3. Add more cloud shapes for fur around the neck, on the legs and on the end of the tail. Fill in the paws and the nose.

# Scruffy mongrel

Add little lines by the tail.

1. Draw an oval for the head. Add an oval snout. Add lines and ovals for ears on top. Add the nose and a tongue.

2. Draw a body. Add stick legs and a curved stick tail. Then, draw shaggy fur on the ears and over the eyes.

3. Add more shaggy fur on the rest of the body and the tail. Add some fur to the snout. Fill in the nose.

Draw the dogs in pencil, then use felt-tip pens to outline them and fill them in.

# Adding shading

Adding shading to your drawings can create highlights and shadows that make them look three-dimensional. Pencil is good for shading because it's easy to make it lighter or darker. When you shade, use the side of your pencil's lead and do lots of parallel lines, close together. Press gently for light shading. For dark shading, press firmly and go over an area several times.

## Choosing a pencil

Pencils come in varying degrees of softness, shown as an 'H' or 'B' number on the side of the pencil. H stands for hard and B stands for black.

An HB pencil is a medium hardness pencil. It is good for drawing outlines and doing light shading.

Use light shading for well-lit areas.

Use dark shading for shadowy areas.

White highlight

A 2B pencil is quite soft. It is good for smooth, dark shading.

You can use a soft putty rubber to create white highlights.

Pull a piece off the putty rubber and roll it between your fingers. Dab it over your drawing to lift off the pencil.

## Shading textures

Skin is usually smooth. For smooth shading, press gently and build up dark tones slowly. For a very smooth effect, blend your pencil marks by rubbing them with a finger tip or cotton bud, but don't overdo this.

Smooth shading

Blended shading

Hair and clothes often have rough textures. You can use dots and lines to create textured shading.

Use short lines for rough, hairy skin or fabric.

Use criss-cross lines for a woven texture.

Use dots for freckled skin or stubbly hairs.

Use squiggly lines for curly hair or furry fabric.

# Coloured pencils

Coloured pencils are good for making delicately coloured drawings. You can use them to create either textured or smooth areas of colour.

# Colour shading

Shading with coloured pencils is similar to shading with ordinary pencils. The strength of a colour depends on how hard you press. You can also blend different colours together by shading them on top of each other. Some coloured pencils are water-soluble. This means that their lead dissolves in water (see below).

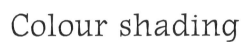

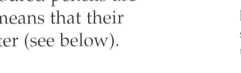

Use criss-cross lines, dots and squiggles to create texture on clothes.

If you press hard, you get a dark, strong colour.

If you press lightly, you get lighter, softer colours.

To use water-soluble pencils, dip a brush in water and paint over your shading.

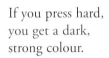

Water-soluble pencils can be blended with water for a soft, painted look.

For delicate skin tones, press gently as you shade and build up colours gradually.

This olive colour is a blend of brown, green and orange.

Add blue to make colours darker – this dark brown is a blend of light brown and blue.

This pinkish skin tone is a blend of orange, yellow and brown.

# Shading ideas

This page shows you different ways of using pencils for filling in and shading your pictures.

## Solid shading

The strength of your shading depends on the softness of the pencil you are using and how hard you press. See page 36 to find out which type of pencil to use.

If you press hard, you will get a strong, dark shade, like on this dragonfly's body.

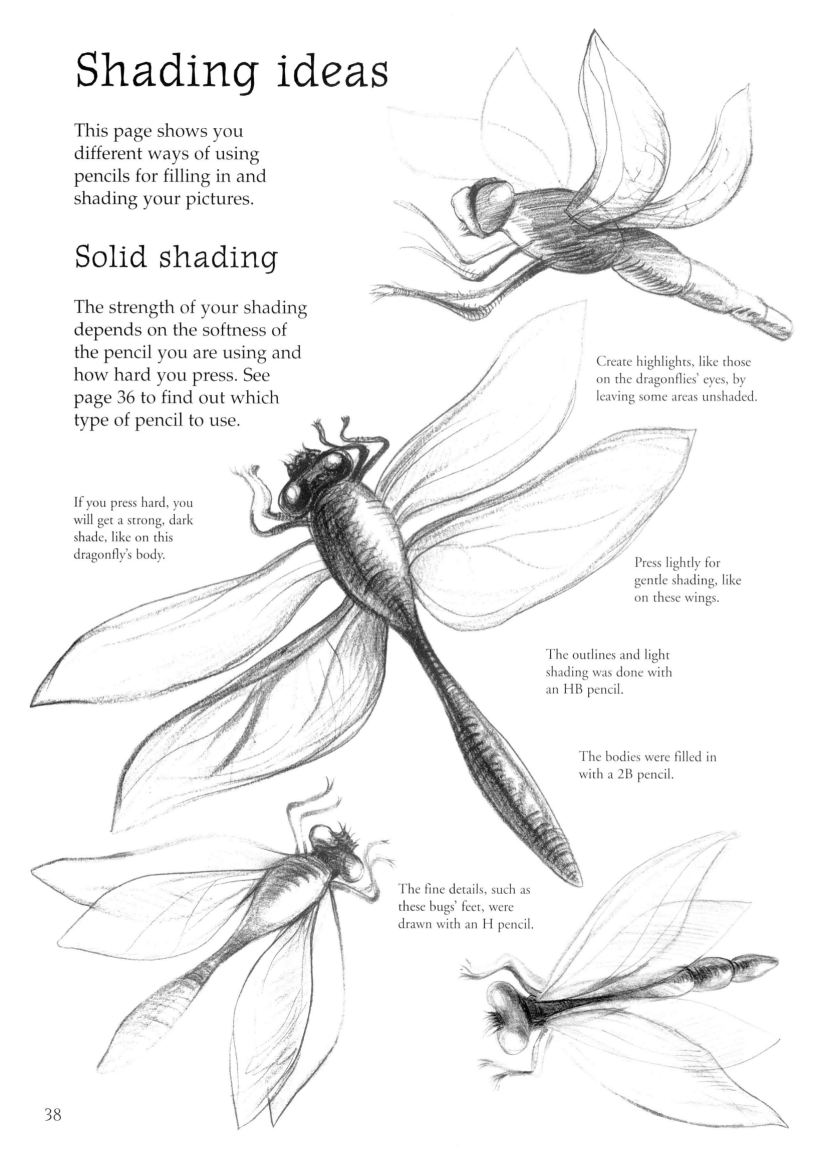

Create highlights, like those on the dragonflies' eyes, by leaving some areas unshaded.

Press lightly for gentle shading, like on these wings.

The outlines and light shading was done with an HB pencil.

The bodies were filled in with a 2B pencil.

The fine details, such as these bugs' feet, were drawn with an H pencil.

# Other effects

You can create different types of shading by filling in shapes with different patterns or marks. Use a thin felt-tip pen to experiment with some of the ideas here.

Draw lots of parallel lines next to each other, like on the bird's beak. This is called hatching.

Draw lots of lines at one angle, then do more lines across them. This is called cross hatching.

Cross hatching

The strength of shading depends on the distance between the hatched lines.

Fill a shape with lots of dots. If you draw them close together the shading will look darker.

Shading with dots is called stippling.

Fill a shape with lots of spirals. They are good to show curly hair or fur.

# Pencil bugs

1. Use a pencil with a soft lead (a 6B pencil is ideal) to draw a simple outline of an insect on your paper.

2. Shade the insect's body, making it darker close to the edges. Fill in the head and legs. Add any spots or patterns, too.

3. Rub lines across your drawing with an eraser to smudge the pencil a little. Rub the lines in different directions.

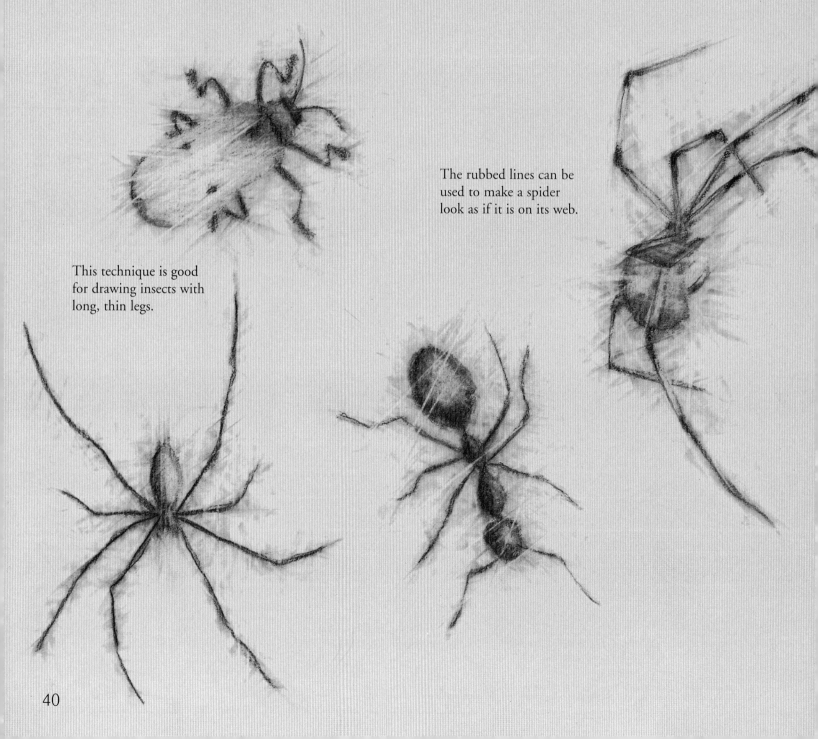

The rubbed lines can be used to make a spider look as if it is on its web.

This technique is good for drawing insects with long, thin legs.

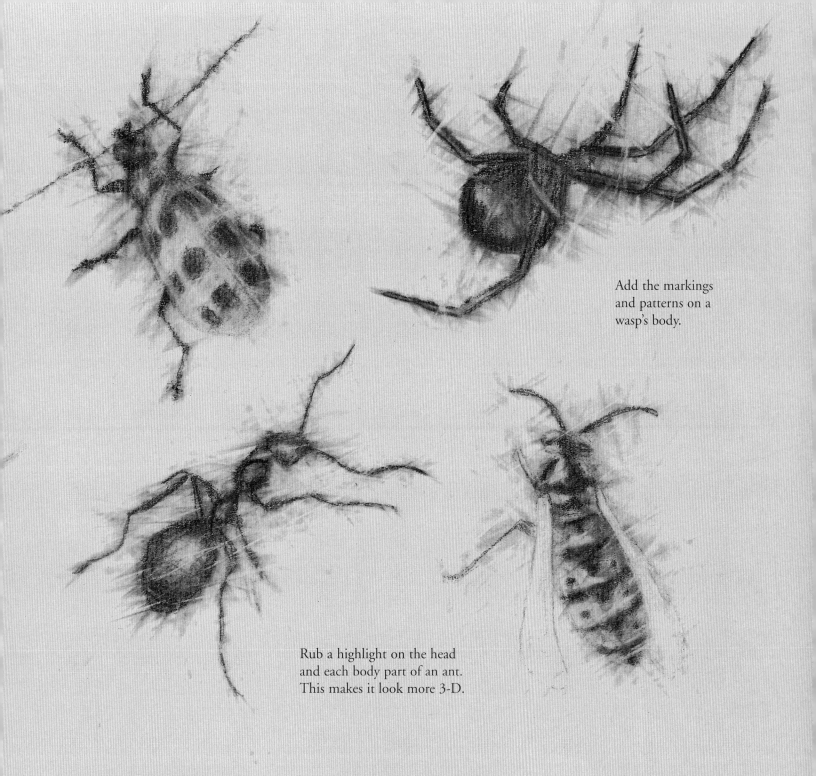

Add the markings
and patterns on a
wasp's body.

Rub a highlight on the head
and each body part of an ant.
This makes it look more 3-D.

4. Use a harder pencil, such as a 2B, to draw over the insect again. Add shading and details to it too.

5. Rub lines over the drawing again, but be more careful this time. You just want to smudge the lines a little.

6. Then, use the eraser to rub away some of the pencil shading to create a shiny highlighted patch on the insect's body.

# Drawing with pastels

Oil pastels give you very bright, strong colours. They don't smudge in the way chalk pastels do. This makes them easier to use. Chalk pastels are very soft and they smudge easily. This means that you can get some great effects by mixing and blending them.

Like chalk pastels, oil pastels work well on coloured paper which has a slightly textured surface.

Try doing short strokes in the same direction in different colours.

Use chalk pastels on their sides to fill in areas of colour. Peel off the paper and break them in half, first.

Try doing lots of overlapping strokes in different colours.

You can draw on black paper with oil pastels, although the colours you get may change slightly.

A white oil pastel shows up well on brightly coloured paper.

## Mixing colours

To mix colours, use one colour on top of another (see the tiger opposite). The colours blend together.

Oil pastels work well on cartridge paper and sugar paper.

# A tiger in long grass

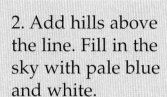
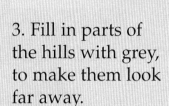

1. Draw a straight purple line about a third of the way down the paper.

2. Add hills above the line. Fill in the sky with pale blue and white.

3. Fill in parts of the hills with grey, to make them look far away.

4. Use the side of an orange pastel to fill in the foreground.

5. Draw the outline of a tiger on top of the foreground.

6. Add patterns on the fur with orange, yellow and black.

7. Let the black stripes blend with the other colours where they overlap.

8. Draw lots of long grass in front of the tiger with greens and brown.

# Oil pastel lizards

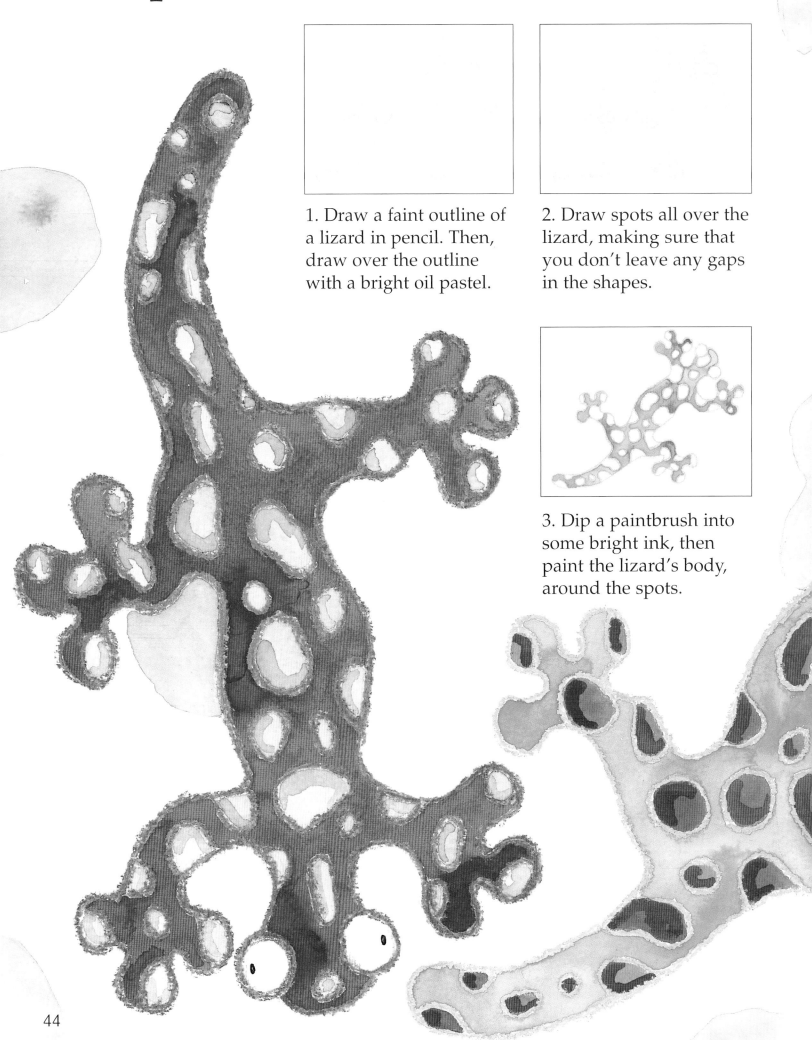

1. Draw a faint outline of a lizard in pencil. Then, draw over the outline with a bright oil pastel.

2. Draw spots all over the lizard, making sure that you don't leave any gaps in the shapes.

3. Dip a paintbrush into some bright ink, then paint the lizard's body, around the spots.

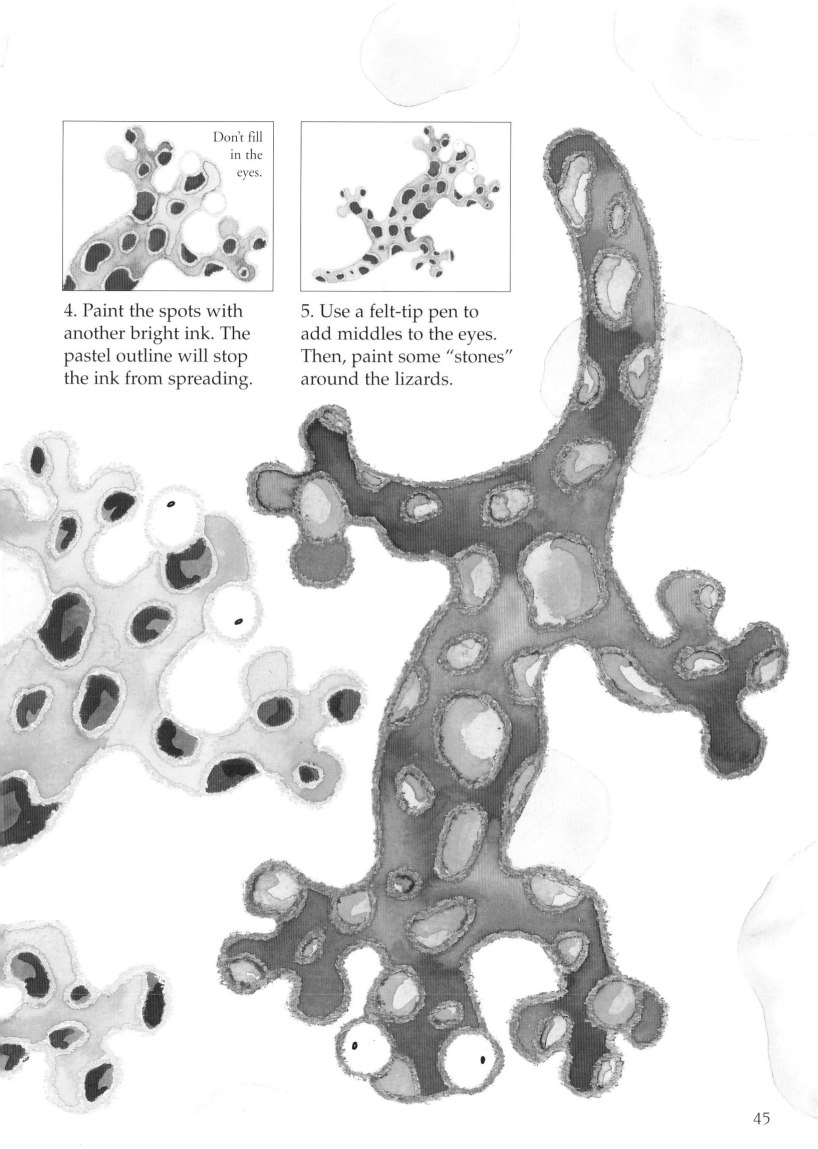

4. Paint the spots with another bright ink. The pastel outline will stop the ink from spreading.

Don't fill in the eyes.

5. Use a felt-tip pen to add middles to the eyes. Then, paint some "stones" around the lizards.

# Chalky polar bears

You can draw these polar bears using chalk pastels to get a soft, furry effect. The bears' white fur and their snowy surroundings mean you only need black and white chalk pastels to create the picture.

Chalk pastels work well on coloured paper.

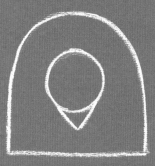

Leave room for another bear on the right.

1. With a white chalk pastel, press lightly and draw shapes like these for the first polar bear. Draw them quite big.

2. To the right of the first bear, draw the shapes for the second one. Make its nose overlap the first bear.

The neck slopes down here.

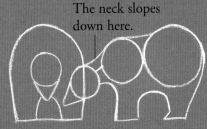

3. Draw the bears' outlines around the shapes with smooth, curved lines. Add arches for their legs.

Take care around the overlapping nose.

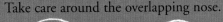
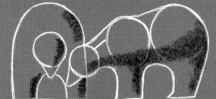

4. Use a small piece of black chalk pastel on its side to fill in some dark areas on the two polar bears, like this.

Rest your hand on a scrap of paper to avoid smudging your picture as you draw.

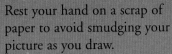

5. Use a white chalk pastel on its side to colour the light areas. Go right up to the black parts with the white colour.

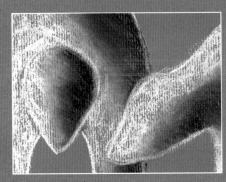

6. Using your finger, gently smudge the black and white together where they meet. The smudged bit will go grey.

7. To show the bears' fur, do short, slanted lines in black all over the grey areas, and also around the black edges.

46

8. In white, do more slanted lines in the grey areas and also around the white edges, to show the fluffy white fur.

9. Do a little black mark for each eye and semicicles for the ears. Colour the tips of the noses in black.

Go round the ears in white.

10. Draw some hills in black and white. Add shadows under the bears' feet. Blend them gently with your finger.

Blue paper helps the scene look icy and cold.

The bears' shadows are like blurry reflections.

# A pastel fantasy landscape

1. Draw two curved bands, using a black chalk pastel.

2. Fill in the space between the bands with a dark blue pastel.

3. Add a band of yellow, then another band of dark blue.

4. Fill in with diagonal strokes of black and ultramarine blue.

5. Do long white strokes on top of the bands of black, to make grey.

6. Blend all the colours with your finger or a cotton bud.

7. Wash your hands or use several cotton buds. They will get dirty.

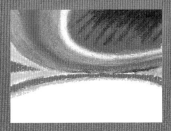

8. Then, draw a grey line. Add red and yellow stripes above it.

9. Draw different sizes of circles and lots of wavy lines in the foreground.

The paper protects your picture.

10. Lay a piece of scrap paper over the bottom part of your picture.

11. Draw moons and stars in the sky. Then, gently blend them in.

12. Draw clouds on the horizon with grey or a mixture of black and white.

13. Use yellow to add a wavy highlight along each cloud.

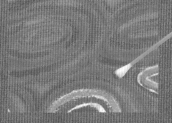

14. Blend the foreground, but leave the clouds as they are.

49

# Hairy orangutan

Chalk pastels can be used to show different kinds of texture. For example, you can blend two or three colours together to show an orangutan's skin, and you can use unblended lines to show the long hair on its body.

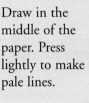

Draw in the middle of the paper. Press lightly to make pale lines.

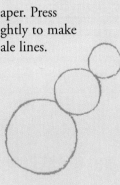

The circles line up diagonally.

1. With an orange chalk pastel, draw three circles on green paper, as shown here.

Hand

Elbow

Shoulder

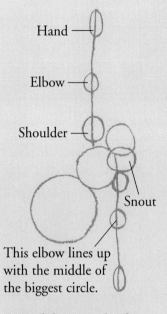

Snout

This elbow lines up with the middle of the biggest circle.

2. Add a circle for the snout. Draw lines for arms, then add circular joints and oval hands.

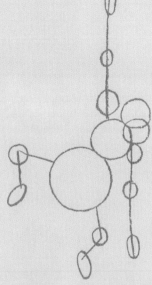

3. Draw two bent lines for legs. Then, add circular knees and oval feet.

These fingers curl around the branch.

Add a branch in brown pastel.

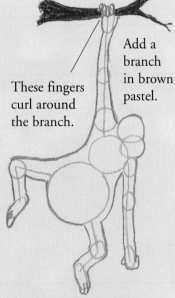

4. Draw the outline, like this, going around the arms and legs. Add fingers and toes.

Blow on the paper to get rid of any pastel dust.

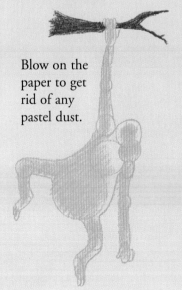

5. With a pale orange pastel, fill in these areas. Blend them in with your finger.

Smudge the dark areas to the edges of the light ones.

6. Fill in the dark areas with a brown pastel. Blend them in with your finger.

7. Add hair with orange and brown pastels. Use long lines and don't blend them.

8. Add a little pink on the face, chest and belly and blend it in with your finger.

50

Try drawing
a line of
swinging
orangutans.

Draw a pale
line along the
top of the
branch for
a highlight.

The fingers and toes
were outlined with the
tip of a black pastel.

9. Add some pale
pink lines for
highlights on the
arms, face, legs,
and feet.

10. With a black
pastel, draw eyes
and nostrils. Draw
a line for the mouth
and add the ear.

# Oil pastel effects

Use oil pastels in two different ways to create these bright butterflies.

## Stained glass effect

Draw the outline in pencil first if you want to.

 Press hard.

1. Fold your paper in half, then open it out. Draw half a butterfly with a black oil pastel.

2. Fold the paper in half again, then rub all over one side with the handle of a pair of scissors.

3. Unfold the paper. Use the pastel to draw over the faint outline of the other half of the butterfly.

4. Draw leaves in the background. Paint inks in the sections between all the outlines.

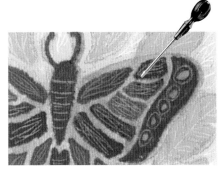

# Ink outlines

Leave a gap between each section.

1. Follow steps 1-3 on page 52, but use a pencil to draw the outline. Fill in the spaces between the outline with oil pastels.

2. Paint all over your picture with a bright colour of ink. It will fill the gaps between the coloured sections.

3. Use the edge of a screwdriver to scratch details on the butterfly's wings and on the leaves in the background.

# Wax crayons

Wax crayons can be used in lots of different ways. You can get lots of shades with one crayon by varying the amount of pressure you use. You can also mix them to make different colours. They are also good for doing rubbings and resist effects.

This shows some different shades you can get when you vary the pressure as you draw.

You can also mix wax crayons, although they don't blend together as well as chalk or oil pastels.

## Wax resist stars

Press hard.

1. Draw stars all over your paper. Use two colours for each star. Add a trail from each star.

2. Mix up lots of dark blue watercolour paint in a pot. Don't make it too thin and watery.

3. Brush the paint across the paper, covering your drawing. The crayon resists the paint.

# Fantasy bird

1. Draw a large bird with a pencil. Press lightly to get a faint outline.

Look at the big picture to see the white lines to draw.

2. Draw feathers on the head, body and tail with a white wax crayon. Draw lines on the feet, too.

3. Mix up some orange paint in a pot. Paint all over the picture.

4. Use a fine brush to paint details on the body and head. Use dark red paint.

5. Add more details to the feathers using the dark red paint.

6. Paint around the eye, beak and feet. Add stripes to them.

55

# Wax resist fish and butterflies

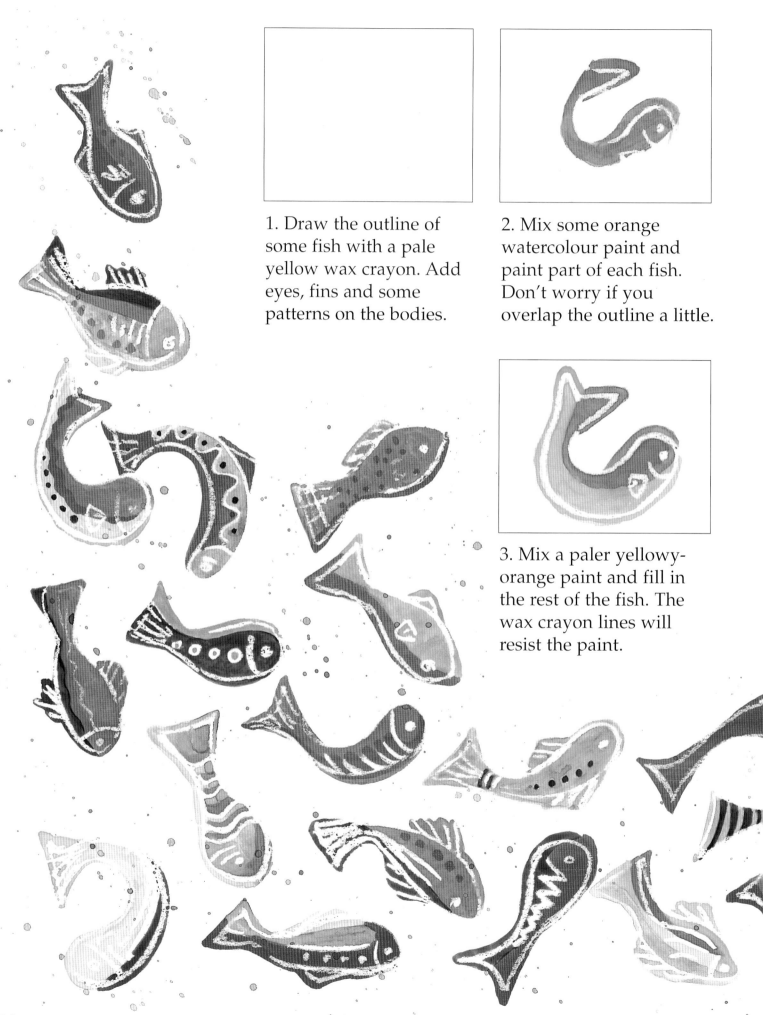

1. Draw the outline of some fish with a pale yellow wax crayon. Add eyes, fins and some patterns on the bodies.

2. Mix some orange watercolour paint and paint part of each fish. Don't worry if you overlap the outline a little.

3. Mix a paler yellowy-orange paint and fill in the rest of the fish. The wax crayon lines will resist the paint.

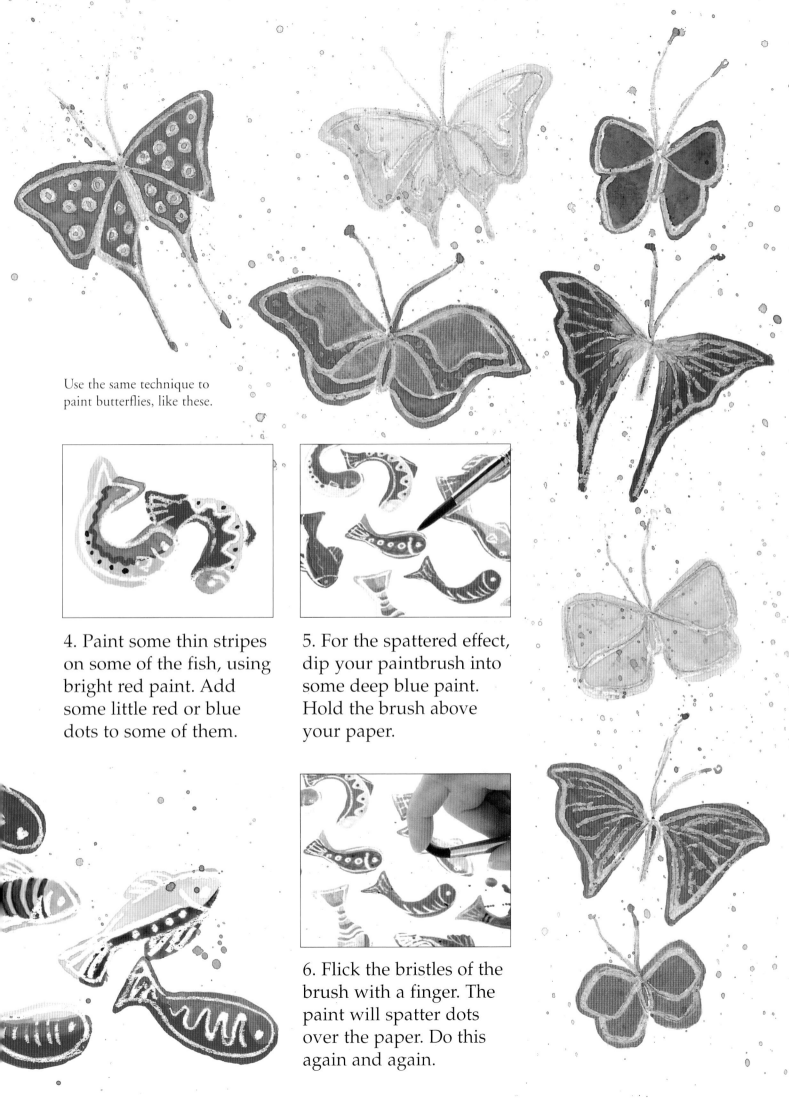

Use the same technique to paint butterflies, like these.

4. Paint some thin stripes on some of the fish, using bright red paint. Add some little red or blue dots to some of them.

5. For the spattered effect, dip your paintbrush into some deep blue paint. Hold the brush above your paper.

6. Flick the bristles of the brush with a finger. The paint will spatter dots over the paper. Do this again and again.

# Waxy zebras

Zebras are quite similar in shape to horses (see pages 66-67). When you look at a four-legged animal from an angle, the legs furthest from you look higher up or shorter. This is called perspective. You can use the technique shown here to draw horses or other four-legged animals from this angle.

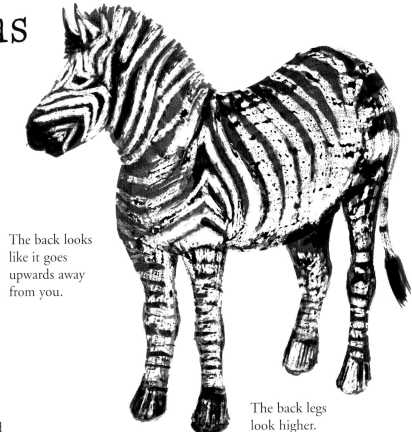

The back looks like it goes upwards away from you.

The back legs look higher.

These zebras were drawn in pencil, then filled in using white wax crayon and black ink.

The grass below was drawn with wax crayon then yellow watercolour was painted on top.

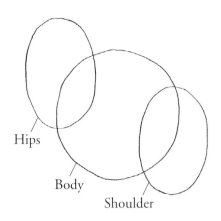

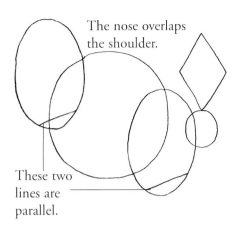

The nose overlaps
the shoulder.

These two
lines are
parallel.

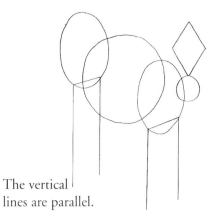

The vertical
lines are parallel.

Hips

Body

Shoulder

1. In pencil, draw an oval for the hips, a circle overlapping it for the body, and another oval for the shoulder.

2. Draw a diamond and an oval for the head and nose. Draw two slanted lines inside the shoulder and hip ovals.

3. Draw four lines, one for each leg, coming from each end of the slanted lines. The lines for the legs should be parallel.

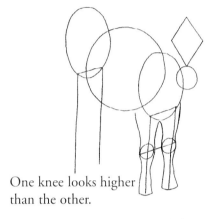

One knee looks higher
than the other.

4. Draw a line parallel to the shoulder line, halfway down the front legs. Add the knees and then outline the legs.

5. Draw a line parallel to the hip line, halfway down the back legs. Add knee circles, and then outline the back legs.

6. Draw the rest of the outline. Add a tail. Then, rub out the extra shapes and lines inside the outline.

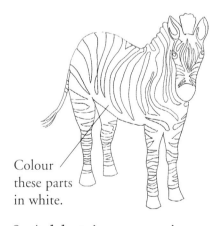

Colour
these parts
in white.

If the ink sticks to the wax stripes, scrape it off with your fingernail.

7. Add the zebra's ears, eyes and mane. With a thin, white wax crayon, put a dot in each eye for a highlight.

8. Add stripes, curving them around the body. Colour the white parts in wax crayon. Add white bits to the hooves.

10. Paint watered-down black ink all over the body. Most of it will run off the wax, letting the white parts show.

# Drawing trees

These pages show you different ways of drawing and painting trees. When you try any of these techniques, you will get a better result if you make your tree bigger than the ones shown.

## Oil pastel trees

This tree was filled in with dots, instead of short lines.

1. Draw a twisted tree trunk using dark brown oil pastels. Add several short branches.

2. Draw lots of short diagonal lines with a green oil pastel, overlapping the branches.

3. Add more diagonal lines for the leaves, using a lighter green and a lime green pastel.

For autumn leaves on a tree, use orange, brown and rusty-coloured pastels.

# Pen and ink

1. Use brown ink to paint a very simple trunk with three thick branches coming from it.

2. Use green ink to paint a wavy line for the top of the tree. Then fill it in, leaving some small gaps.

3. Use a felt-tip or an ink pen to draw loopy lines around the edge of the tree and around the gaps.

# Brushed branches

1. Paint a patch of green and brown watercolour paint. Spatter it by flicking the bristles of your brush.

2. Leave it to dry, then use different shades of brown watercolour paint to paint the trunk.

3. While the trunk is still wet, paint the branches by brushing the paint up onto the leaves.

# Chalk pastel leaves

1. Paint a trunk with yellowy-brown watercolour paint. Add some branches, too.

2. Draw lines using a light green chalk pastel. Add some darker green lines on top.

3. Gently rub the tip of your little finger down the lines to smudge the chalks together.

# Drawing feathers

Birds' feathers can be speckled or spotted, striped or plain. On this double page there are a few techniques for drawing and painting birds and feathers.

To do a feather, start by painting a simple feather shape, like this.

Look at real feathers to get some ideas.

These spots were printed with an eraser on the end of a pencil, dipped in white paint.

Use the tip of a fine brush to paint fine lines on a feather.

The speckles on this feather were drawn first with oil pastels, then watercolour was painted on top.

Draw a feather with a soft 6B pencil, then add stripes with ink.

The stripes on the feather below were added while the ink was still wet.

Use chalk pastels to draw a soft, downy feather.

# Pheasant

1. Paint the body using watery brown watercolour paint. Go over the head, tail, tummy and legs with a darker brown.

2. While the paint is wet, add black and brown dots to the tail and tummy. Paint dark areas on the head, beak and neck.

3. Paint around the eye with red paint. Use a thin felt-tip pen to outline the body, adding feathers to the wing and tail.

# Spotted woodpecker

1. Paint a thick black line for the head, back and tail. Then use finer lines for the rest of the body.

2. Paint a line on the tummy with watery ink. Fingerpaint spots on the tail with acrylic paint.

3. Fill in the body with a peach-coloured chalk pastel. Add markings on the back and wing.

4. Draw a red chalk patch on the head and tummy. Smudge the pastel a little with your finger.

This woodpecker was painted in ink. The branch was drawn with a 6B pencil.

# Drawing fur

Some animals have long hairy fur, curly fur, or smooth skin. They can also be one colour or have amazing patterned fur. Here are a few suggestions of different ways to draw animal fur.

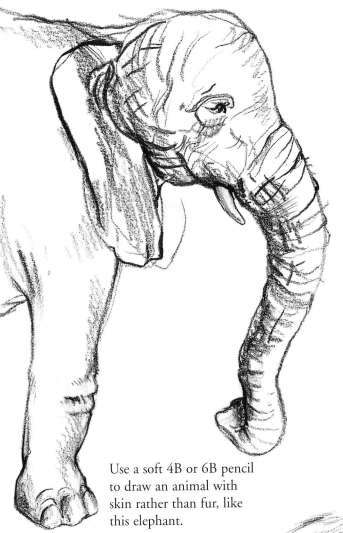

The long fur on these animals called guanacos was painted with lots of thin wavy lines. Shorter, straighter lines have been used on the smooth fur.

Use a soft 4B or 6B pencil to draw an animal with skin rather than fur, like this elephant.

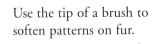

Use the tip of a brush to soften patterns on fur.

For hairy fur, add fine wavy hairs with chalk pastels.

Press harder and harder with a pencil for fur like this.

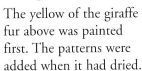

The yellow of the giraffe fur above was painted first. The patterns were added when it had dried.

The spots and hair of this spotty fur were drawn on a patch of orange chalk pastel.

# Pencil and paint

1. Use a soft 6B pencil to draw a lion's eyes, ears and nose. Add some curved lines for the mane.

2. Paint lines in shades of orange between the pencil lines, but don't put too much paint on your brush.

Add shading down the side of the face and over the eyes when the paint is dry.

# Chalk pastel leopard

1. Use a pencil to draw a faint outline of a leopard on coloured paper. Fill in its nose and eyes and add some long whiskers.

2. Using a chalk pastel, fill in areas on the leopard's head, along the neck and back, and down the legs and tail.

3. Use a darker pastel to fill in shadows under the chin and on the tail, legs and tummy. Smudge the pastel with a finger.

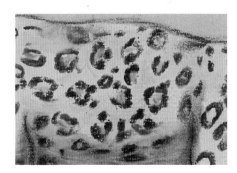

4. Add spots on the head, back, tail and legs. Then, outline the leopard and its eyes and nose with a black pastel.

# Drawing horses

Horses can be quite tricky to draw. A good way of getting the proportions right is to compare the length of the animal's head with other parts of its body as you draw it. As you follow the steps below, try using the horse shown here to help you to get the shape right.

The blue lines on this horse are all the same length.

This shows how long different parts of the horse's body are compared to its head.

Draw this lightly in pencil.

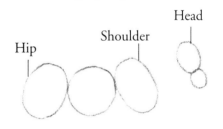

Head

Shoulder

Hip

1. Draw a circle, with a slanted oval either side for the shoulder and hip. Draw two more ovals for the head.

The zigzags start from the centre of the ovals.

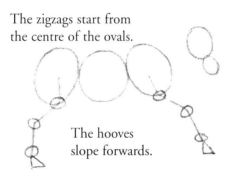

The hooves slope forwards.

2. Draw zigzag legs from the shoulder and the hip. Add circles for the joints. Then, add triangles for the hooves.

The back dips here.

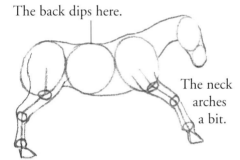

The neck arches a bit.

3. Draw the outline around the shapes, like this. When you have finished, rub out any lines you don't need.

4. Add an ear pointing backwards. Rub out the part of the neck that overlaps it. Then, add the eye and nostril.

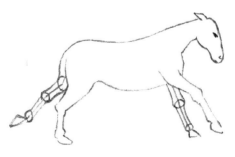

5. Draw two more zigzags for the other legs. Add hooves. Then, outline the legs and rub out the lines inside them.

The tail flows from the backbone.

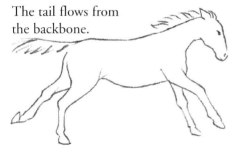

6. Draw the mane and tail using a few long lines. They are streaming out behind the horse to show its movement.

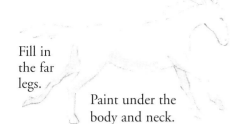

Fill in the far legs.

Paint under the body and neck.

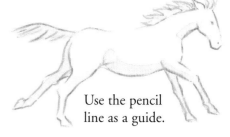

Use the pencil line as a guide.

7. Mix some blue ink with lots of water to make a pale shade. Paint it in the places shown here to show the horse's shape.

8. Paint the pale blue in long, flowing lines to show the mane and the tail. The brush marks can go outside the lines.

9. When the horse is dry, go over the outline in blue pencil. Vary the pressure on the pencil to get thick and thin lines.

Blue ink was flicked from a paintbrush around the horses' feet to make it look like they are galloping through water.

The shadows beneath the horses' feet were added before the flicked ink.

67

# Kangaroos in motion

Animals are difficult to draw in motion but can make the most exciting pictures. If you draw an animal's legs using a zigzag line, you can just change the shape of the zigzag to draw the legs in different positions.

The zigzag changes shape as the kangaroo moves.

Chalk pastels were used to draw these kangaroos.

Press very lightly.

Press harder for the back and tail.

1. Draw a big oval and a smaller oval for the kangaroo's body. Add a circle for the head with a wedge-shaped muzzle.

2. Draw a curve for the back and the tail. Add a big zigzag for the back leg and a smaller one for the front leg.

3. Draw an outline around the head shapes. Add the ears. Then, draw the rest of the outline, adding the legs and tail.

Lay a piece of scrap paper over the parts you have drawn to protect them, while you do the rest of your drawing.

The lines overlapping the outline give a sense of speed.

Your shading can go outside the outline a little.

Do all the lines in the same direction.

4. Use an orange chalk pastel to draw lots of lines all going in the same direction. Leave some paper showing through.

5. Use a paler chalk pastel to add highlights on the kangaroo's back, tail, legs and on the head.

6. Use a darker chalk pastel to add the details to the face. Then, add shadows under the body, legs and tail.

# Animals in action

As well as drawing animals in the poses shown in this book, you might want to draw them in other positions. Use these drawings as reference to help you.

## Dog

Sleeping

Sitting

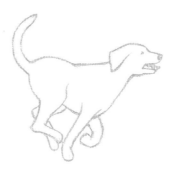

Running

Jumping

## Cat

Sleeping

Sitting

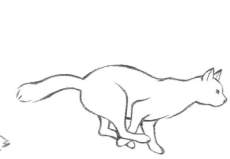

Running

Jumping

## Rabbit

Grazing

Sitting up

Cleaning

Hopping

These animals have been shaded with smudged chalk pastels.

# Horse

Grazing

Trotting

Rearing

Jumping

# Polar bear

Sleeping

Walking

Rearing

Standing

# Monkey

Sitting

Climbing

Running

Swinging

71

# Birds in flight

You can use the same basic shapes to draw birds in lots of different flight positions. Draw a seagull following the steps below. Then, use the flight positions to help you draw more seagulls and create a whole scene.

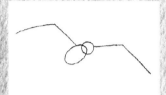

1. In pencil, draw an oval body and a circle for a head. Draw lines to position the wings.

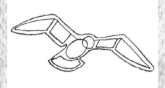

2. Then, draw the wing shapes. Draw the tail. Then draw the whole outline.

3. Rub out the extra lines inside the outline. Add the bird's eyes, the beak and feet.

## Flight positions

When near the ground, a bird might drop its head and let its feet hang down.

When gliding, a bird straightens its wings and tucks in its feet.

When landing, a bird tilts its wings and drops its feet.

From the front, the body looks short and the wings look narrow.

## Painting the scene

Leave the colour uneven to look like clouds.

1. Dampen the paper around the birds with a brush. Then, paint a blue watercolour sky.

2. When the sky is dry, use pale grey watercolour to paint shadows on the birds.

3. With black watercolour, paint the eyes, and the tips of the wings and the tails.

4. Mix a bit of orange watercolour. Paint the beaks and feet of the birds. Let them dry.

# Bird shapes

An eagle has very long, broad wings.

A swallow has angular wings and a forked tail.

A jay's body and wings are quite short.

You can draw different types of birds using similar shapes to those used for drawing seagulls.

73

# Drawing a face

Although no two faces are exactly the same, all faces have the same basic shapes. These shapes are shown on the photograph below. Follow the steps on these pages to draw a face using guidelines.

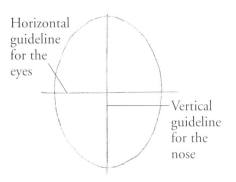

Horizontal guideline for the eyes

Vertical guideline for the nose

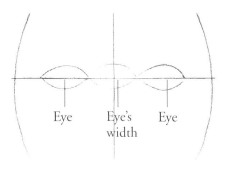

Eye

Eye's width

Eye

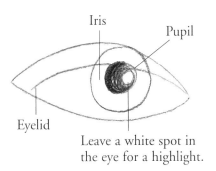

Iris

Pupil

Eyelid

Leave a white spot in the eye for a highlight.

1. Draw an oval in pencil. Add a faint line down the middle of the oval. Add another faint line across the middle.

2. Draw two almond shapes for the eyes. Position them on the horizontal guideline, an eye's width apart.

3. Draw a circle in each almond, for the iris. Add an overlapping line for the eyelid. Draw a small circle for the pupil and fill it in.

The distances and guidelines marked on this photograph work for almost every face.

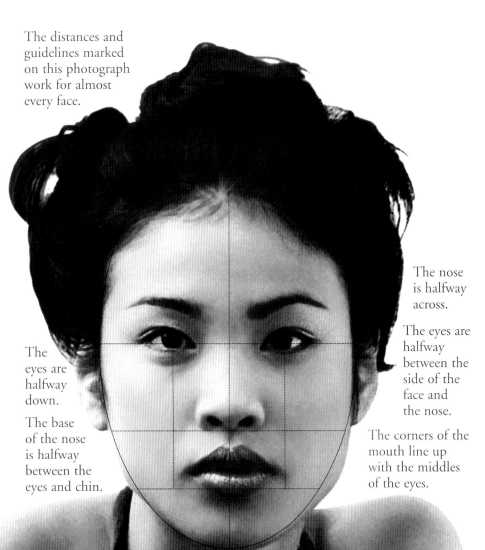

The eyes are halfway down.

The base of the nose is halfway between the eyes and chin.

The nose is halfway across.

The eyes are halfway between the side of the face and the nose.

The corners of the mouth line up with the middles of the eyes.

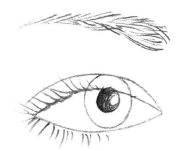

4. Draw the lashes and eyebrows. Make your pencil lines follow the direction in which the hairs grow.

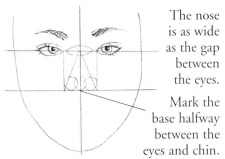

The nose is as wide as the gap between the eyes.

Mark the base halfway between the eyes and chin.

5. The nose is on the vertical guideline. Draw a triangle for the nose shape. Add three overlapping circles at the base.

6. Outline the circles to make the sides and bottom of the nose. Add two oval shapes for the nostrils and fill them in.

Draw lines to make sure things line up.

Bottom lip

7. Draw the bottom lip halfway between the nose and chin. Make the corners line up with the middles of the eyes.

8. Draw a flattened-out 'm' shape for the top lip. Add another flatter 'm' shape for the line between the lips.

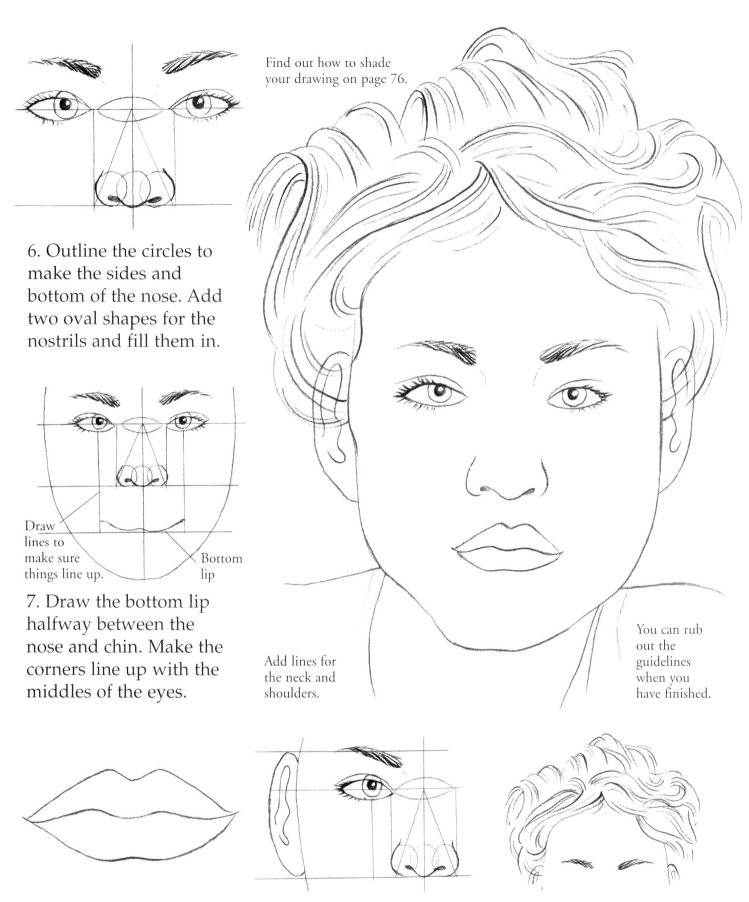

Find out how to shade your drawing on page 76.

Add lines for the neck and shoulders.

You can rub out the guidelines when you have finished.

9. Draw the ears, making them level with the eyebrows at the top and the nose at the bottom. Add a curved shape inside each.

10. Draw the hairline above the eyebrows. Then, draw the rest of the hair, making your lines follow the way the hair falls.

# Shading faces

Once you have drawn a basic face shape, you can try adding shading. This creates the highlights and shadows that make your drawing look three-dimensional.

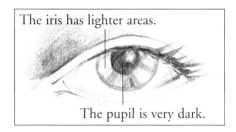

The iris has lighter areas.

The pupil is very dark.

1. Shade around the eye with a 2B pencil. Then, shade the iris with lines coming out from the pupil. Shade the pupil, leaving a tiny, white highlight.

Highlight

2. Shade the lips with short pencil strokes, making the top lip darker than the bottom one. Use a rubber to add a highlight on the bottom lip.

3. Add dark shading around the base of the nose. Lightly shade the sides of the nose. Then, blend this shading into the shading around the eyes.

4. Shade around the tip of the nose, leaving a highlight on the tip itself. Shade the creases at the corners of the mouth and the hollow underneath it.

5. Shade lightly around the edge of the face and add a dark shadow under the chin. Then, fill in the hair with wispy pencil lines.

Lightly shade the neck, too.

# Coloured pencil drawing

For this drawing, you can use normal coloured pencils or water-soluble pencils without any water. This style of drawing is often used for fashion designs, so look through some fashion magazines for some ideas and different faces to draw.

The highlights in the eyes were left uncoloured.

You can add touches of pink on the cheeks.

Use a strong colour on the lips to look like lipstick.

1. Draw an oval in light blue pencil. Don't press too hard. Add the features. Try drawing the irises to the right, so the eyes look sideways.

2. Draw the hair in light blue. Draw around the sides of the face and one side of the nose in brown. Add the eyebrows.

3. Sharpen the brown pencil and draw dark lines along the top of the eyes. Draw in the irises and pupils, too.

4. Lightly shade the face in light brown. Add some darker brown down one side of the face and under the chin.

5. Shade the lips in red. Add brown on the top lip, to make it darker. Fill in the hair with long, flowing pencil lines.

# Dramatic lighting

Lighting can completely change how someone looks – all-round lighting makes a face look flat, while side lighting, shown below, casts strong shadows and can make a face look mysterious. Black and white chalk pastels are good for drawing this dramatic lighting effect.

1. Find a picture of a face with strong lighting on one side, or ask a friend to pose for you, with a desk lamp shining towards one ear.

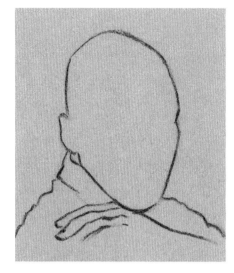

2. On a piece of beige or grey paper, use the tip of a black pastel to outline the head and shoulders, making them fill the paper.

3. Draw in the features with the tip of the pastel. If you make a mistake, you can rub it out with a putty rubber or smudge it away.

4. Break off a small piece of pastel and use the side of it to shade around the dark side of the face, down the side of the nose and under the mouth.

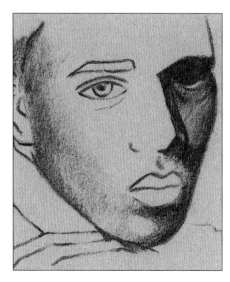

5. Shade lightly around the light side of the face. Where you stop, rub the shading with a finger tip so it blends with the colour of the paper.

6. Shade lightly around the eye, nose and mouth on the light side of the face. Shade the upper lip so it is just slightly darker than the paper.

7. Add a little white pastel on the light side of the face, on the cheek and forehead. Rub the white pastel so it blends with the paper.

8. Shade the background and hair with strokes of black pastel. Let the strokes overlap the dark side of the face, so it blends into the shadows.

9. Add dark details, like the lashes and nostrils, with the tip of the black pastel. Add white highlights in the eyes, and on the nose and lips.

The fingers have white highlights on top and dark lines underneath. There is a shadow on the back of the hand.

# Drawing side views

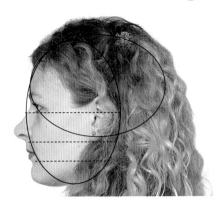

A side view, or profile, of a face looks quite different from a front view. These pages show you how to draw a side view using guidelines, and how to make silhouettes.

## A side view

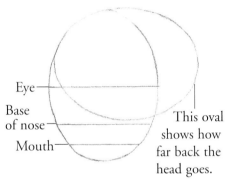

Eye

Base of nose

Mouth

This oval shows how far back the head goes.

1. Draw an oval and mark horizontal guidelines for the eye, nose and mouth (see page 74). Draw a second oval, the same size, on its side like this.

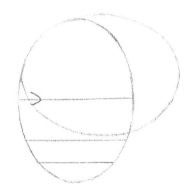

2. For the eye, draw a 'v' shape on its side. Position the 'v' on the guideline for the eye, about a quarter of the way across the first oval.

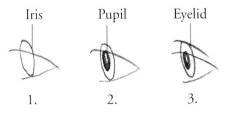

Iris    Pupil    Eyelid

1.    2.    3.

Shade the pupil, leaving a small, white highlight.

3. Draw an oval for the iris of the eye, making it overlap the top of the 'v'. Add an oval pupil. Draw a line at the top of the iris, for the eyelid.

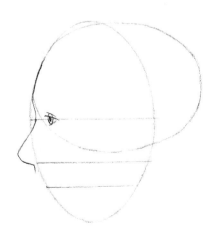

4. Draw the forehead, making it curve inward level with the eye. Add the nose, making the base of the nose level with the guideline for the nose.

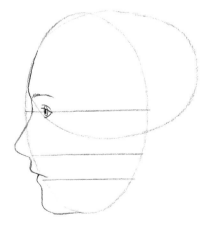

5. Draw the lips and chin next. The lower lip slopes back slightly from the upper one. Then, draw in the eyebrow over the eye.

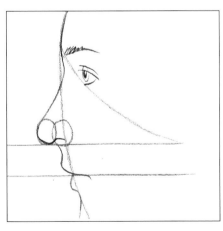

6. Draw two overlapping circles at the base of the nose. Draw a line from the left circle curving up across the second circle, to form the nostril.

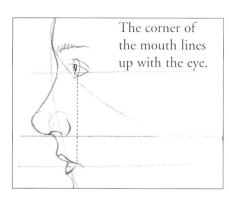

The corner of the mouth lines up with the eye.

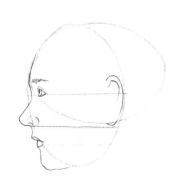

7. Draw the mouth with two curved lines for the lips. The top lip is thinner than the lower lip. Add a line slanting down between the lips.

8. For the ear, draw a curved shape at the edge of the first oval. The ear lines up with the eyebrow and nose. Add a line inside the top of the ear.

9. Draw a hollow inside the ear. Add the hair and neck. Rub out your guidelines and carefully go over the main lines of your drawing again.

# Silhouettes

A good way to compare different people's profiles is to make silhouettes (cut-out shapes) like the ones shown below.

1. Tape some paper to a wall with masking tape. Sit a friend in front of it. Place a lamp so the profile casts a shadow on the paper.

2. Draw around the shadow in pencil. Then, take the paper down and carefully cut around the shape you have drawn.

Try making silhouettes of other friends in different colours. Put them together like this to compare them.

# Drawing cartoon bodies

In cartoons a character's body can be whatever shape you want it to be. Here are some tips for drawing cartoon people's bodies. You can vary the shapes to get different characters.

This picture was drawn with felt-tip pens and painted with watercolours.

## Body proportions

Cartoonists can vary the body proportions of their characters to create different effects. For example, the bigger the head looks in proportion to the body, the cuter or more child-like the character will look.

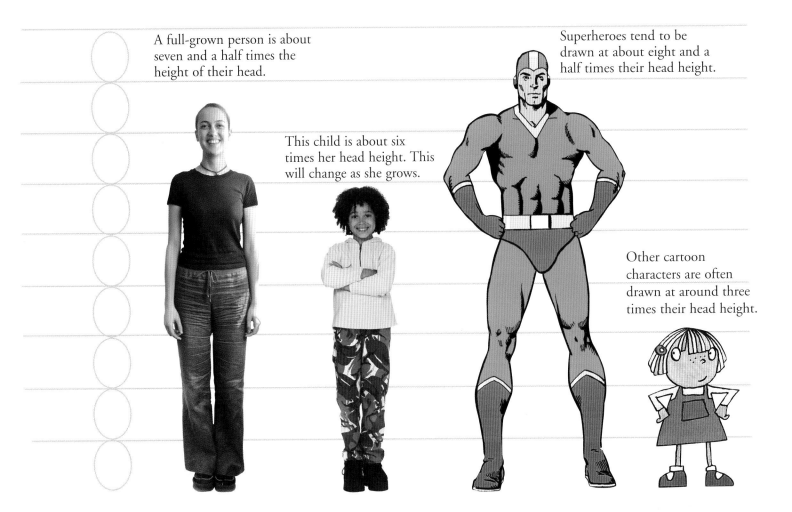

A full-grown person is about seven and a half times the height of their head.

This child is about six times her head height. This will change as she grows.

Superheroes tend to be drawn at about eight and a half times their head height.

Other cartoon characters are often drawn at around three times their head height.

# Body building

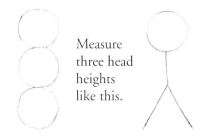

Measure three head heights like this.

1. In pencil, draw a circle for the head and then a line for the body. Add two stick legs coming from the body.

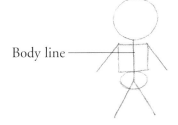

Body line

2. Add a rectangle for the ribs and an oval for the hips. The legs start halfway through the hip oval. Add stick arms.

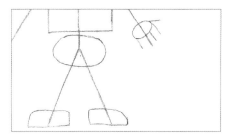

3. For the hands, draw ovals and add stick fingers and thumbs. Then, add feet to the bottoms of the stick legs.

4. Draw a face and hair using techniques and ideas given on pages 8 and 9. Add two lines for the neck.

5. Draw a T-shirt and trousers. Then, outline the arms and the hands. Use curved lines for the hands and fingers.

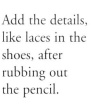

Add the details, like laces in the shoes, after rubbing out the pencil.

6. Go over the outline using a felt-tip pen. Leave it to dry, and then rub out all the pencil lines inside the figure.

Use the step-by-step instructions above, but vary how big you draw each part to get different body shapes.

This robot is short and squat. Try drawing a tall, gangly one too.

To draw an older child, make the arms and legs longer.

A gorilla has very long arms and short legs.

# Moving bodies

To draw a person from different angles you have to make them look three-dimensional. To do this, you can draw construction lines in pencil to help you get everything in the right place. You can erase these when the drawing is finished.

## Turning faces

Construction lines drawn on an orange can help you to see how the eyes, nose and mouth move when a face moves into different positions. The facial features always stay in the same position in relation to where the lines cross.

You can use these photos of a face on an orange as reference for how to draw a face in different positions.

Facing the front, the construction lines look straight.

Draw a circle. Add two construction lines making a cross inside. Then add the eyes, nose, mouth and ears.

Looking to the side, the vertical line looks curved.

Draw a circle. Add the construction lines, making the vertical line curve to one side. Then, add the face.

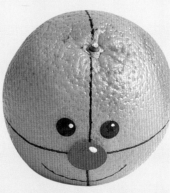

Looking down, the horizontal line looks curved.

Draw a circle. Add the construction lines, making the horizontal line bend downward. Then, add the face.

Looking upward, the horizontal line looks curved.

Draw a circle. Add the construction lines, making the horizontal line bend upward. Add the face.

Looking down and to the side, both lines look curved.

Draw a circle. Add the construction lines, making both the horizontal and the vertical lines bend. Then, add the face.

84

# Turning bodies

To draw a body from different angles, you can use similar techniques to those used for the head. Here are some tips.

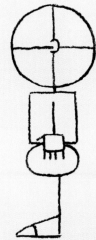

Use the shapes on page 83 to draw a body from the front. To draw shoes from the front, draw a triangle and then add a semicircle for the toe.

To draw someone turning slightly, draw a slanted square for the body. Add arms to the top corners. Draw triangle shapes for the feet.

From the side, one arm moves to the middle of the body shape, in line with the spine. The nearest leg completely overlaps the one further away.

From the back, the body shapes look similar to those from the front. But only the backs of the ears show, and the feet are triangles without the toe shapes.

# Focus on hands and feet

These drawings show you hands and feet from various angles. You can use them as reference to help you.

Hands

Feet

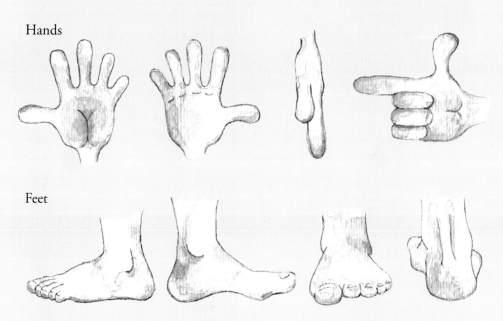

# Superheroes

Superheroes have special powers, which can be anything from superhuman strength, to being able to fly or change their shape. They are normally seen battling villains. These pages give you a starting point for drawing superheroes of your own.

## Drawing a superhero

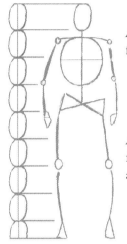

Add circles for joints.

Add triangles for hands and feet.

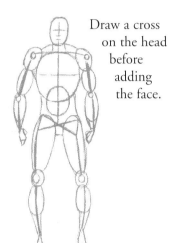

Draw a cross on the head before adding the face.

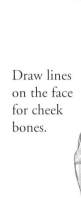

Draw lines on the face for cheek bones.

1. Draw an oval head and a stick body. Add an oval chest. Draw the hips, arms and legs. Make the figure eight and a half times its head height.

2. Add ovals for bulging muscles to the arms and legs. Add an oval for the stomach muscles. Outline the shoulders and waist.

3. Go over the outline. Draw the face. Add gloves, boots and pants. Add dark areas for shading in the places shown here to emphasize his muscles.

## Poses

The secret to making superheroes look dramatic and exciting, is to draw them in very exaggerated poses. The stick men below show some action poses you could use.

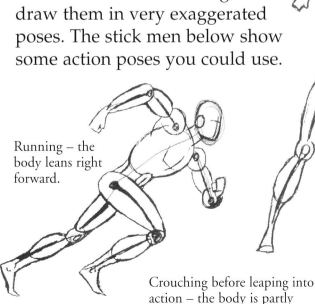

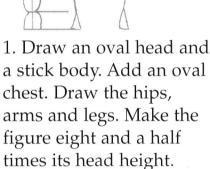

Running – the body leans right forward.

Running forward – the body leans forward and the head looks up.

Flying – the body forms a straight line.

Crouching before leaping into action – the body is partly hidden behind the legs.

Swinging a punch – the body twists to one side.

# Chasing and racing

There are tricks you can use in your drawings to show things moving. Motion lines are the most common technique, but you can also add puffs of dust and words, or use a blurring effect to show movement.

## Zooming car

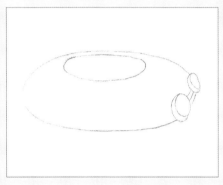

These are motion lines.

1. Draw an oval car body. Add another oval for the opening in the top. Draw headlights and a grill at the front.

2. Add slanted oval wheels. Add a character inside the car, leaning forward, and holding a wheel. Add the bumpers.

3. Drawing quickly, add two downward strokes behind the car and by each wheel. Draw horizontal lines from the back.

This race was outlined in pen and then painted using watercolours. The techniques described above were used to show the speed of all the racers.

A number was added to each racer, so they look like they are in an official race.

# Blurred legs

1. Draw an oval head with long ears. Add a stick body leaning forward. Draw an oval on it. Add an arm and a tail.

2. Draw a scribbly oval where the legs would normally go. The legs are moving so fast they look like a blur.

3. Drawing quickly, add some motion lines at the bottom of the blurred legs. Then, add some little puffs of dust.

# Sound effects

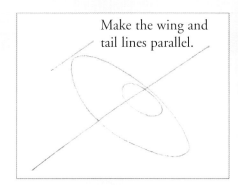

Make the wing and tail lines parallel.

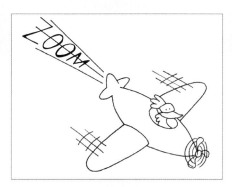

1. Draw an oval body for the plane. Add an oval cockpit. Pressing lightly, add diagonal lines for the wings and tail.

2. Outline the wings and tail. Add a character inside the cockpit. Add the propeller with scribbly circles on it.

3. Draw lines from the back of the plane. Then write 'zoom' inside the lines. Add motion lines behind the wings.

# Perspective

The further away things are from you the smaller they look. This is called perspective. There are tricks you can use to show perspective in your drawings to make them look three-dimensional.

In this cartoon, the path gets smaller and smaller into the distance until you can't see it any more. The point at which it disappears from view is called the vanishing point.

Horses and a cowboy were added to make a Western street scene.

This is the vanishing point.

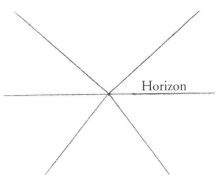

1. Draw a horizontal line for the horizon. Then, add four slanted lines coming from one point on the horizon.

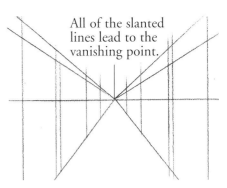

All of the slanted lines lead to the vanishing point.

2. Add vertical lines for the walls of each building. Add more slanted lines for the tops of the buildings.

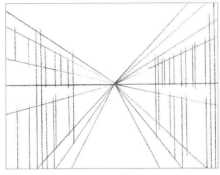

3. For the windows and doors, draw more slanted lines from the vanishing point. Then, add vertical lines for their sides.

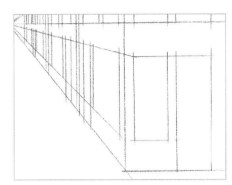

4. Draw horizontal lines for the fronts of the buildings on the street facing you. Add windows and doors.

Add a line here to show the wall.

5. Add a pavement line and roofs to the buildings. Shape the doors, windows and fronts of the buildings.

6. Add frames around the windows and doors. You can add details, such as awnings on shop fronts and tiles on roofs.

# Skewed views

If you want to show something from a person's point of view, you can warp the drawing so that it looks like you are seeing it from a certain angle. This is another way of showing perspective (see page 90).

## Worm's eye view

If you were very small and you looked up at a very tall person, such as this giant, his body would seem to get smaller and smaller the further away from you it became.

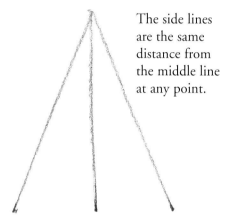

The side lines are the same distance from the middle line at any point.

1. Using a pencil, draw a vertical line. Then, draw two diagonal lines coming from the same point at the top.

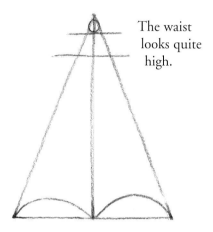

The waist looks quite high.

2. Draw two semicircles at the bottom. Then, mark a line for the waist and shoulders. Draw in a small circle for the head.

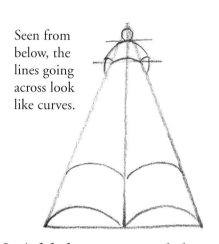

Seen from below, the lines going across look like curves.

3. Add the arms, and draw the shirt sleeves. Draw the curved waist line and shoulder line. Add curved trouser bottoms.

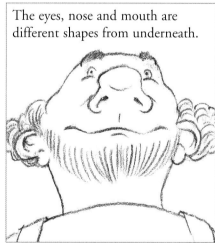

The eyes, nose and mouth are different shapes from underneath.

4. Draw eyes high on the head. Add the nose. Draw a mouth and add ears level with it. Add hairs on the chin and the head.

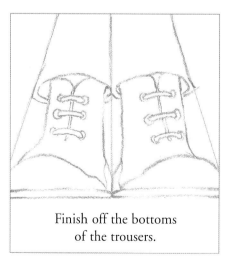

Finish off the bottoms of the trousers.

5. Add lines to show the soles of the shoes. Draw the sides of the boots. Add laces across and then draw the eyelets.

Add a pen outline and rub out the pencil lines.

Add a small character whose viewpoint you are sharing.

# Bird's eye view

If you could look down on a giant from above his head, his body would seem to get smaller and smaller, the further away from you it became.

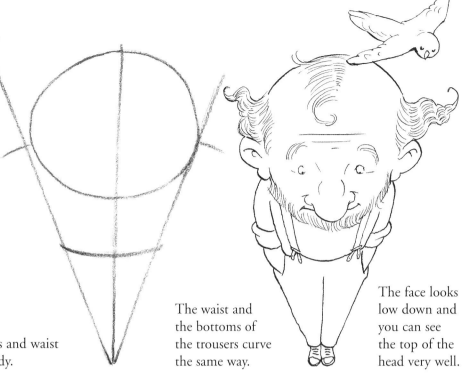

The guidelines for drawing a person from a bird's eye view are the opposite way around from those for drawing a worm's eye view.

Mark where the shoulders and waist go before drawing the body.

The waist and the bottoms of the trousers curve the same way.

The face looks low down and you can see the top of the head very well.

# A giant and a mouse

You can use these two viewpoints to alternate between a short character and a tall character in a comic strip.

# Drawing from life

To get ideas for how people or animals act or look in certain situations, it is a good idea to keep a little sketchbook with you. Make quick drawings of people around you at bus stops, in shopping centres, in parks or playgrounds.

Try to make quick drawings of the way people run.

Don't worry about drawing very accurately, sometimes a rough sketch can show more character.

Do scribbly drawings of the things people do while waiting for a bus.

People standing at a bus stop can look bored, cold, relaxed or tense.

If you are drawing someone close up, make sure you ask their permission first.

# Drawing sleepy pets

If you have a pet, then you can practise drawing it again and again. A good time to draw animals is when they are asleep because they will be keeping quite still.

1. Draw some simple shapes and a rough outline of the animal's pose, first.

2. Add more detail to the outline once you have drawn the whole shape.

3. If the animal moves, you can look at details, like its whiskers, and draw them.

# Drawing groups

When drawing a group of animals, look at different animals in the group to catch their poses. If there's a whole group of ducks for example, you can look at lots of different birds to draw one, as they will all repeat the same poses.

Draw the animals in the front larger and with more detail than the ones in the background. Also, make the background ones paler.

# Index

animals,
  animal characters, 34-35
  animals in action, 70-71
  birds in flight, 72-73
  brush and ink drawings, 22-23
  brush paintings, 28-29
  chalky polar bears, 46-47
  drawing feathers, 62-63
  drawing from life, 94-95
  drawing fur, 64-65
  drawing horses, 66-67
  drawing with pastels, 42-43
  hairy orangutan, 50-51
  head-on hippos, 30-31
  ink and pastel pets, 18-19
  inky panda, 24-25
  kangaroos in motion, 68-69
  light and dark, 26-27
  oil pastel lizards, 44-45
  pencil bugs, 40-41
  shading ideas, 38-39
  watercolour giraffe, 10-11
  wax crayons, 54-55
  wax resist fish and
    butterflies, 56-57
  waxy zebras, 58-59

bodies,
  drawing cartoon bodies, 82-83
  drawing from life, 94-95
  moving bodies, 84-85
  skewed views, 92-93
  superheroes, 86-87

buildings,
  domed buildings, 12-13
  perspective, 90-91
  watercolour city, 16-17

cars,
  chasing and racing, 88-89
  dip pen drawings, 14-15

cartoons,
  animal characters, 34-35
  chasing and racing, 88-89

drawing cartoon bodies, 82-83
drawing simple faces, 8-9
moving bodies, 84-85
painting scenes, 32-33
perspective, 90-91
skewed views, 92-93
superheroes, 86-87

chalk pastels,
  a pastel fantasy
    landscape, 48-49
  chalky polar bears, 46-47
  dramatic lighting, 78-79
  drawing feathers, 62-63
  drawing fur, 64-65
  drawing trees, 60-61
  drawing with pastels, 42-43
  hairy orangutan, 50-51
  ink and pastel pets, 18-19
  inky beetles, 20-21
  kangaroos in motion, 68-69

faces,
  adding shading, 36-37
  dramatic lighting, 78-79
  drawing a face, 74-75
  drawing side views, 80-81
  drawing simple faces, 8-9
  moving bodies, 84-85
  shading faces, 76-77

ink,
  brush and ink drawings, 22-23
  brush paintings, 28-29
  dip pen drawings, 14-15
  domed buildings, 12-13
  drawing feathers, 62-63
  drawing horses, 66-67
  drawing trees, 60-61
  ink and pastel pets, 18-19
  inky beetles, 20-21
  inky panda, 24-25
  light and dark, 26-27
  oil pastel lizards, 44-45
  watercolour city, 16-17
  waxy zebras, 58-59

insects,
  brush paintings, 28-29
  inky beetles, 20-21
  oil pastel effects, 52-53
  pencil bugs, 40-41
  shading ideas, 38-39
  wax resist fish and
    butterflies, 56-57

oil pastels,
  drawing trees, 60-61
  drawing with pastels, 42-43
  oil pastel effects, 52-53
  oil pastel lizards, 44-45

perspective,
  perspective, 90-91
  skewed views, 92-93

shading,
  adding shading, 36-37
  dramatic lighting, 78-79
  light and dark, 26-27
  shading faces, 76-77
  shading ideas, 38-39

trees,
  drawing trees, 60-61

watercolour,
  birds in flight, 72-73
  domed buildings, 12-13
  head-on hippos, 30-31
  oodles of doodles, 6-7
  painting scenes, 32-33
  watercolour city, 16-17
  watercolour giraffe, 10-11
  wax crayons, 54-55
  wax resist fish and
    butterflies, 56-57

wax crayons,
  wax crayons, 54-55
  wax resist fish and
    butterflies, 56-57
  waxy zebras, 58-59

Digital Vision © Pages 74, 78, 81, 82.
First published in 2006 by Usborne Publishing Ltd., 83-85 Saffron Hill, London, EC1N 8RT, England www.usborne.com